THE FINGERPRINTS OF GOD

THE FINGERPRINTS OF GOD

Tracking the Divine Suspect through a History of Images

ROBERT FARRAR CAPON

WILLIAM B. EERDMANS PUBLISHING COMPANY
GRAND RAPIDS, MICHIGAN / CAMBRIDGE, U.K.

Published 2000 by Wm. B. Eerdmans Publishing Co.

255 Jefferson Ave. S.E., Grand Rapids, Michigan 49503 /

P.O. Box 163, Cambridge CB3 9PU U.K.

Printed in the United States of America

05 04 03 02 01 00   7 6 5 4 3 2 1

Library of Congress Cataloging-in-Publication Data

ISBN 0-8028-4768-4

ISAIAH 45:15

Verily thou art a God that hidest thyself,
O God of Israel, the Saviour.

(King James Version)

אָכֵן אַתָּה אֵל מִסְתַּתֵּר אֱלֹהֵי יִשְׂרָאֵל מוֹשִׁיעַ׃

(Biblia Hebraica Stuttgartensia)

σὺ γὰρ εἶ θεός, καὶ οὐκ ᾔδειμεν ὁ θεὸς τοῦ Ισραηλ σωτήρ

(Septuagint)

Vere tu es Deus absconditus Deus Israel salvator.

(Vulgate)

Contents

Bibliographical Note

M ost of the passages I've quoted from Irenaeus's *Against the Her-esies* have been taken from *The Ante-Nicene Fathers,* vol. 1, translated by A. Cleveland Coxe (Eerdmans, 1973).

Most of the passages from Athanasius's *On the Incarnation of the Word* have been translated by me from *Athanasius de Incarnatione,* edited by Frank Leslie Cross (SPCK, 1963).

In addition, a few passages from Irenaeus and Athanasius, as well as all the passages from Anselm, Luther, and Calvin, have been quoted from *Documents of the Christian Church,* edited by Henry Bettenson (Oxford University Press, 1959). Passages attributed to Melanchthon are either from Bettenson or from the Augsburg Confession; the quotations from Dame Julian of Norwich have been taken from *Revelations of Divine Love* (Methuen & Co. Ltd., 1949).

A word about the scriptural quotations in this book. Sometimes I've used the KJV, RSV, or NRSV translations without change; but in many cases I've either adapted them by retranslating individual words or phrases or given a translation that is entirely my own. In all cases, the biblical references have been cited and can be looked up in any version you choose to consult.

Finally, since the Divine Suspect has not only left his finger-prints on objective history but has also had a personal history of preferring images to all other ways of leaving his marks on creation, the next few pages contain a slightly whimsical index to many of the images, metaphors, and word-pictures (both biblical and my own) that you'll find throughout the book. I provide this for your possible amusement and/or edification; but whether it achieves either, neither, or both of those, at least I had fun preparing it.

Index of Images

PROLOGUE

Where It All Began

Let me tell you how God redeemed the world.

On the eve of the Big Bang, over single-malt scotch and cigars, the Father, the Son, and the Holy Spirit were making a final run-through of their plans for the event. The Son was enthusiastic. "I think we've nailed it," he said to the Father. "I'm going to speak everything into being as your Word, and the Spirit here is going to breathe life into it. Then the two of us toss it back to you, and the cosmic party dances itself right into our Trinitarian lap. Elegant! *Tov meod! Kala lian! Valde bona,* and all that!"

"I have a problem, though," the Spirit says. "I'm the one responsible for the PR in all this, especially when it comes to the fail-safe gambit of Incarnation we've planned to cover both creation and redemption. The Son really does make the world, right? But with the human race locked into time and space, it's going to look as if we haven't seriously tried to redeem the mess they've made until Jesus shows up late in history. The fact that we've had the Son in there tidying things up from the beginning is the last thing they'll think of. How do I convince them the Incarnation isn't just an afterthought?"

"Easy," says the Father. "Sure, it will look as if the Incarnation of my Word is simply a response to sin. But since all three of us will have been intimately present to everything from square one, all you have to do is give them images that show both creation and redemp-

1

tion going on full force from the start. From before the beginning, in fact, since we're talking about it right now. What's the problem with that?"

"The problem," the Spirit explains, "is precisely with the images. However many mysterious, right-brain images of the Word's age-long presence I give them, they're going to dream up transactional, left-brain ones and view him as something you inserted late in the day. Think of the damage they can do to your reputation as the Father who creates or even to the Son's, as the one who redeems if they decide to think of you as the coach in a football game and the Son as the quarterback. Since you're not going to reveal the Word's Incarnation until some two-thirds of history has gone by, how do I stop them from thinking you kept him in the locker room until the fourth quarter? We three may know he's been in there right from the first possession, but no one else will. Even your biggest fans are going to be hard put to sell that as brilliant management."

"Listen," the Father says. "I decide what's brilliant management, not the fans. And as for my reputation, that's your department, not mine. Besides, haven't we talked about this practically forever? You know the drill. All through the process of revealing my Son in history, you keep slipping them images of the hiddenness of his Incarnation — of the mystery of the Word's activity in the world even before you arrange for him to be born of Mary. You're going to hang images like the Paschal Lamb and the Rock in the Wilderness in their minds. After that, all you'll have to do is get somebody like Paul to say that those things were presences of Christ before Christ — that the Lamb and the Rock are in fact my Incarnate Word anticipating himself. What's so hard about that?"

"Plenty," the Spirit answers. I've been doing simulations of human thought in my mind. I think we've underestimated the effects of cooping people up in four dimensions. Look at it from my point of view. You plunk Jesus into the world at one spot in history, and then you expect me to convince them he's present as your Word in all of history — before, during, and after Jesus?"

The Son interrupts him. "But I really am going to be present. Or, to put it their way, I really will have been all along. So I don't see . . ."

The Spirit's patience is wearing thin. "Give me a break! Since I'm the one who has to take everything that's yours and get it across to them, I'm trying to solve your problems here too. Just think about what they'll do with a Jesus who stays in history for only thirty-three years. Even if I get John to say that he's the Word who made everything from the beginning, they'll probably imagine him as a pot of holy soup we delivered too late for a good many of our customers. And after they've jumped to the conclusion that the Word wasn't present to anyone who lived before Jesus, they'll leap to the even more dreadful notion that nobody who lived after him can have his benefits until their assorted churches get him canned, marketed, and distributed to them."

The Father tries to break in. "But what about the Pentecost party we've planned to get the church going? Won't that . . . ?"

"I'm sorry," the Spirit insists, "but I'm afraid Pentecost will be just one more thing for them to misread. Don't get me wrong: I'm totally on board with both of you. But suppose I do give you the rushing mighty wind and the party hats made out of fire. Even suppose I throw in the mystery of speaking in different languages in order to get the universality of the Son's work into the picture. They're still going to think the church is in the world to sell clam chowder to customers who never had it before.

"I mean, think of the possibilities for ecclesiastical arrogance. Jesus takes away the sins of the world, right? In him, everyone who ever lived gets free forgiveness for whatever went wrong in full, in advance, and all in one cosmic shot, no strings attached. I'm even going to get the church to include "one Baptism for the forgiveness of sins" in the Nicene Creed so they'll see that the Baptism of Jesus himself does the whole job, even if no one else ever gets baptized. But do you know what they're going to do with that? They're going to paint themselves into a corner and say that the unbaptized go to hell or even that sins after Baptism make forgiveness flake off like a bad paint job, and that unless Christians go to confession for a second coat before they die, they'll go to hell too. Oh, sure. We've also agreed on this Reformation business where I convince them that nobody has to do anything to be forgiven except trust the grace that Jesus has already given everybody. But give them a hundred years after that and they'll manage to turn faith itself into a requirement for grace: no faith, no forgiveness. Out the window again goes the free gift we've given them once and for all; and back in comes forgiveness as a deal that's good only as long as they behave themselves."

"But why on earth," the Son wonders, "would they balk at getting something for nothing like that? Free grace and dying love isn't enough for them? Would they rather we dealt with them on the basis of accountability?"

The Spirit just keeps pressing his point. "I don't understand it any better than you do; all I know is what my simulations tell me. Human beings aren't afraid of accountability; they're crazy about it. If they can't get credit for themselves or dish out blame to others, they cry "Unfair!" That's why I pleaded with you to let me include something less subtle in the revelation. Remember? I suggested an image of the Son hiding a box of chocolates in every person's house: the gift would be there whether they know it or not, like it or not, believe it or not. Maybe then they'd see that their faith doesn't do anything to get them the chocolates of forgiveness; it simply enables them to enjoy what they already have. If they don't trust the gift, of course, it won't mean a thing to them. But the chocolates will always be there. I was even willing to make them miraculous, just to keep the element of mystery in the mix: no matter how many pieces anyone ate, the box would always be full. I still think it would have been a good idea."

Finally, though, the Father has had enough. "I understand your difficulties," he says; "but after all, somebody's got to be in charge here. In my mind, we've come up with a revelation that does the work of your chocolates without making us look like candy-pushers. The Son and I have every confidence in you. If you want to inspire the odd Christian apologist here or there to come up with images like that, be our guest. As I said, it's your department. But we're coming down to the wire here, so let's call this a wrap. We have a big day tomorrow."

PART ONE

SOME IMAGES
OF THE HISTORY

ONE

The Womb of the Word

F ast forward now. I'm going to take you in one breath from the
bosom of the Trinity to the situation we and the Bible find ourselves in at the beginning of the third millennium.

This book will indeed be about the mystery of creation and redemption that's been in everything from square one, courtesy of the
Father, the Word, and the Holy Spirit. But because their revelation
of that mystery was not only gradual and progressive but eked out
in their own sweet time, let me take my opening cue from the Father's last remark. As one of his odd Christian apologists, I want to
give you an image of my own for the relationship of both the Bible
and the church to the revelation of his Word. It's the image of a
womb.

First, though, I want to insist on the historical inseparability of
Scripture and church. The Bible didn't drop down from the sky into
a hat. It arose out of the experiences of the people of God as a community of faith; and it was written by, among, and for those same
people. Indeed, that community came into being before there were
any Scriptures at all. The Jews leaving Egypt didn't have the book of
Exodus or anything else of the Old Testament; and the first believers in Jesus didn't have a scrap of the New. Still, when the Hebrew,
Greek, and Latin Scriptures finally did appear, one form or another
of the word *church* was in them all.

In the Hebrew, we find *qahal* and *edah* ("assembly" and "congregation") as appellations for the people of Israel. In the Greek version of the Old Testament (called the Septuagint and abbreviated as LXX in honor of the seventy Jewish scholars who are said to have prepared it), those Hebrew words were translated as either *ekklēsia* or *synagōgē*. And in the Latin version (the Vulgate), they were commonly rendered as *ecclesia* — which eventually wandered into English as "church." If you happen to wonder why first-century Jewish believers — all of whom saw themselves as the fulfillment of the assembly and congregation of Israel in Jesus the Messiah — ended up using the Greek word *ekklēsia* instead of *synagōgē* as the most common name for their church, I think I can tell you. They did so first of all because they were intimately familiar with the Greek of the LXX (perhaps even more so than with the Hebrew Scriptures); and second, they did so because even before their life as the *ekklēsia* got going, the alternative Greek word *synagōgē* had already been used as the name of an existing institution within Judaism.

Nevertheless, in both the Old and the New Covenants, the church was a *womb,* a *matrix* in which the Word of God himself gestated and from which he was delivered in written manifestations over a long period of time. And once any of those Scriptures came into being, the inseparable duo of church and Bible became an *ongoing womb,* a joint matrix in which the creating and redeeming Word continued to gestate — and still continues to be born — right up to the present day. But since that analogy may strike you as a bit of a stretch, let me justify it for you. I say that the Word of God was gestating in the church because of the two times in the history of the people of God to which I've already alluded. Let me spell them out a bit more fully.

The band of slaves who realized their identity as the *edah* of Yahweh in the Passover and at the Red Sea may well have had some stories about their ancestors in oral tradition; but in 1250 B.C., when that church of the Old Covenant first set foot in the wilderness of Sinai, it had no written documents at all. The books of the Law (the Torah, from Genesis through Deuteronomy) were yet to come; and so too was all the rest of the Hebrew Bible: the Historical books, the Prophets, the Psalms, and the Writings. The only items the community of wanderers possessed were the staves in their hands, the unleavened bread in their sacks, the clothes on their bodies, and the jewelry they had "borrowed" from their Egyptian neighbors on the way out. True enough, the creating, saving mystery of the Word of God himself was fully present to them in the Paschal Lamb, for example, or in the Pillars of Cloud and Fire, or in the Rock in the Wilderness. But the Word of God Written in Scripture was present only *in utero*. It was still gestating, waiting for the later days of its delivery.

The same thing can be said about the church of the New Covenant. On the feast of Pentecost, when that apostolic congregation of faith realized its identity as the renewed *ekklēsia* of Israel, it didn't have a word of the New Testament. The letters of Paul, the Gospels, the Catholic Epistles, and the Apocalypse of John were still forming in the matrix of that community. But all through the hundred years or so of its gestation, the Word of God Written was dwelling in the womb of the church just as surely as the Word of God Incarnate was in the womb of the Blessed Virgin for the nine months of her pregnancy. So the New Testament church at Pentecost was in no position (any more than Mary was) to reach inside itself before the season of delivery and consult with the Word Written for guidance. It simply had to trust the presence of the Word in its midst and to wait out (as Mary did) the fullness of his own time.

But even after the Word of God Written finally saw the light of day, the analogy of church and Scripture as inseparable elements of a matrix still held — and still holds today. Strictly speaking, the Bible isn't just a book; it's the *voice* of the Word himself speaking in and to the church. It's the sacrament of a Person really present, not simply a collection of his words faxed in. Unfortunately, though, when people hear the word "Bible" now, they think of a (largely unread) book on a shelf or of a CD-ROM stored in a computer. And if they do look into it, they use it as if it were an owner's manual supplied to them by the Divine Manufacturer of human nature — as something to be consulted when they want answers, not as a constant companion who wants them to learn the right questions. In any case, it's not something they immerse themselves in day and night. If it's just a trouble-shooting book, why should they give it any more time than a Volvo manual they consult only when they have a problem? And by the same token, if they wouldn't join a group that meets to hear lessons from a book written by modern Swedish engineers, why should they bother with a church that gives them sermons from a manual some two millennia out of date?

Still, the "operating instructions" view of the Bible dies hard. Ever since the invention of printing in the fifteenth century, the temptation to see the Bible as a book in the glove compartment has been growing. And now, given the popularity of biblical literalism, many people seem to believe that's the only way to look at it. So much so, that even when some of us do get a glimpse of what it really is — namely, a *story* — we read it as the wrong kind of story. We take it as the narration of occasional interventions by God in human affairs rather than as the mystery story of God's hidden presence as the Divine Suspect behind all of history. We see it as the record of a series of Band-Aids that God put on the wounds of the world, or of medicines that he injected into the body of creation, when in fact it's a record of the fingerprints he's left on times and places to clue us in to the mystery by which he, in the Person of his eternal Word, has always been drawing all of history to himself. It reveals to us the telltale marks of the One who is the cure, not just some ER measures he's taken to patch us up. The Bible is the story of the Divine Physician himself. His treatments are only the way we meet him, not the keys to his success.

Accordingly, since the story is a true mystery as opposed to a mere detective yarn, you have to meet its hidden Protagonist on his terms, not just leap to your own conclusions about what he did or said. And his terms lead you into the heart of mystery. The trouble with almost all the mystery stories you're used to is that they're nothing but puzzles to be solved by plausible explanations. They never lead you deeper into mystery; they simply plunk you back in the same old world of knowable causes and effects that you live in every day. True enough, such stories do provide a certain amount of suspense by hiding pieces of the puzzle until the end. But when you finally do get to the end, it turns out that no real, profoundly paradoxical mystery was ever there; it was all just sensible stuff about which the author had kept you in the dark.

But Scripture, as the ultimate mystery story, works by an entirely different set of rules. From the very start, there's no conventional suspense: you know that everything's going to come up roses in the end. Yet when that ending is finally disclosed, it catapults you into a world that has violated all the rules of the world you know. Foolishness and weakness conquer wisdom and strength; the Word of God Incarnate wins the day by going out of the god business we invented for him; and the whole world goes home free in a festival of divine forgetfulness. But throughout the entire story, the Bible insists that the mind-boggling solution which emerges at last has in fact been in the works all along. And it's a solution that doesn't hinge on the minor characters' dim-witted or recalcitrant responses to the Word; it depends only on the mysterious presence of the Word himself in every one of those bit players, good, bad, or indifferent — and on their presence in him from the foundation of the world.

To put it in theological terms, redemption depends solely on the inner life of the Trinity and on the Incarnation of the Word of God: the reconciliation of all things has always lain hidden in the ordinary being of all things. Or, to put it in more everyday language, heaven is not a matter of choice. Like the spinach soup at the Waldorf, it's served to you no matter what you order. Hell, of course, is a real possibility; but it's only an option of sorts. It's a choice not to trust, to have no faith in the Word who's already holding you in the redeeming soup of the eternal interchanges between the Father, the Son, and the Spirit. And in those interchanges, it's the Word of God himself who is the final Key to the mystery, not your worthiness as a valued customer.

Look at it this way. The Word speaks all things into being at the beginning. But then, when his creatures deface the world by contradicting his speaking (by denying their own natures as he has spoken them), the Word just keeps on talking. At the very instants of their contradictions, without a single throat-clearing or a moment's hesitation, he counterspeaks their contradiction in his same, original voice. In him, creation and redemption are one act; both have always been going on full force in everything. True enough, it took time for Scripture to reveal that gracious gift. But when it's all set down in black and white, grace is its ultimate point. It proclaims that the Word who makes the world is identical with the Word who saves the world, and it says he's always been doing both jobs. No matter how lost the world may get, it's always been found in the mystery of its Maker.

Let me admit right away that the universe into which that mystery thrusts us is not a place you or I would have chosen as our cup of tea. All kinds of questions come up about it. If the Word has tidied up the mess of history from the beginning, why hasn't he exempted the world from having to slog through it? Why does he insist on time, space, and history at all? Why doesn't he just settle for an unwritten novel in his own head where no real beings will have to scream their way through the torture chamber of creation?

There are, of course, no satisfactory answers to such questions. There is only the paradox of the Word's final response: by his Incarnation, he assures us that he's as much in the chamber of horrors as we are. He brings his Divinity down into the misery of our humanity, and he lifts that very misery up into himself. He doesn't simply contemplate the brokenness of the world from on high. On the cross, he breathes his last in the midst of the brokenness he's freely taken on for our sakes: "My God, my God, why have you forsaken me?" He who is the Answer dies as lost as anyone who never found answers. But even then, it's he himself, in the mystery of his lostness, who remains the only Finder of us all.

∿

But perhaps my insistence on the mystery by which the Word of God Incarnate draws all to himself (John 12:32) troubles you. You wonder whether it's the right reading of the Word of God Written. You admit, perhaps, that the Word has made "all things new" (Rev. 21:5); but you wonder how I can thump so hard for everybody's inclusion when so much of Scripture seems to insist on the opposite. You want to ask me, "What about all the passages where exclusion is said to be the lot of the wicked? What about the threats of punishment, temporal and eternal, uttered against the unbelieving? What have you done with the hell we know and love?" My response to you is that I take such passages without a single grain of salt: for me as for you, they're all the Word of God. So yes, there is exclusion in Scripture, and therefore I accept it. And yes, there is a hell of unutterable torment, so I accept that as well. I wouldn't go so far as to say I love it; but I do agree that we have to keep it in our theology. Otherwise, the rotten apples would spoil our eschatological barrel.

None of that, however, is what I'm concerned with here. I want to talk about the broader scriptural problem your questions raise — namely, the matter of contradictions in the Bible. Obviously, there's no way of denying them: they're just there, on points both small and great. But if we try to resolve them on the basis of left-brain images of Scripture, we give ourselves problems above and beyond the contradictions themselves. Consider literalism once more. It imagines the Bible as a box filled with uniformly true propositions, any one of which can be plucked out and given the same weight as the whole boxful. But that's not what it is. It's not a container for truths; it's a story told by the Truth himself. And because it's a story, the Spirit who is its presiding author and editor is free to use all the devices available to any storyteller.

Think about that. The Spirit can certainly use words in their literal sense whenever he wants (as, for example, when he describes David's affair with Bathsheba, or Jesus' crucifixion, or the geographical details of Paul's travels); and he can make all the propositional statements he likes, just as if he were producing a manufacturer's manual (witness the Ten Commandments). But he can and does use dozens of other devices. He can allow something early in the story that he intends to forbid later, and vice versa. (Polygamy is tolerated early on, but monogamy eventually becomes the rule; the death penalty for adultery is commanded in Leviticus but frowned on by Jesus.) Or he can include two flatly divergent accounts of the same action. (In chapter one of Genesis, human beings — the *adam*, male and female — are created all at once on the sixth day; in the second chapter, the same *adam* is created as a single individual and woman is made later from one of his ribs.) Or he can command an entire system of religion for a thousand years (the animal sacrifices of the Tabernacle and the Temple), and then he can abolish that religion altogether after its fulfillment in the death and resurrection of Jesus the Messiah (as he does in the letter to the Hebrews). And for good measure, he can toss in love poetry (the Song of Solomon), epic (Jonah), poetic fiction (Job), worldly wisdom (Proverbs), history (the

13

books of Kings), disagreements between major characters (Peter and Paul), and even whole books whose writers failed to understand the point of other books (James versus Romans and Galatians, or 2 Peter and Jude versus Paul in general).

But the deepest difficulty with literalism is that it fails to see the principal device the Spirit uses to weave all those elements into a single story. All that wildly various wet-wash is hung on a paradoxical clothesline of imagery, not on a string of uniform propositional truths. The Bible is held together by *icons,* by word-pictures like Light, Word, Water, Marriage, the Garden, the Tree, the Blood of Abel, the Paschal Lamb, the Blood on the Doorposts, the Rock in the Wilderness, the Bread from Heaven, and finally the City, both as the historical Jerusalem in the Old Testament and as the destiny of the world in the book of Revelation. It's these icons, these sacraments of the real presence of the Word himself, that make it a whole.

Take what the Spirit does with *water* as the first instance. A good writer can surreptitiously bury an image in the first chapter of a novel and dig it up over and over again throughout the book (as Robertson Davies does at the beginning of his "Deptford Trilogy" when he has a boy throw a snowball with a rock inside it and then, over the course of the entire work, makes it reappear time after time to further the story). So too with the Holy Spirit. Like a skilled novelist, he introduces the image of water in Genesis 1 and proceeds to dig it up repeatedly, advancing the plot of Scripture with each new appearance. Consider. There are the waters above and below the firmament at the beginning of creation and the mist from the earth that watered the whole face of the ground. There are the four rivers in Eden that water the earth and the waters of the Flood in the Noah story. There are the waters of the Red Sea and the water from the Rock in the Wilderness. There are the waters of Jordan in the book of Joshua and those same waters as the Spirit reintroduces them in the Baptism of Jesus. There is the water and blood from his side on the cross, and there is the Living Water of Jesus himself in the Gospel of John.

Or take the Spirit's handling of *light*. "Let there be light!" is the first word God speaks at the creation. In the Gospel of John, the

Word who is God is called the life, and that life is declared to be the Light of all humanity. And in Revelation, the glory of God lights up the heavenly city and the Lamb is its Lamp. Again, consider *tree*. The two trees in Eden are the Spirit's images for God's best and our worst. He gives us the tree of Jesse as the emblem of the messianic line and then portrays Jesus as its ultimate fruit. He has Jesus declare himself the True Vine and us his branches. He brings on the tree of the cross to overcome our disaster at the tree of the knowledge of good and evil. He inspires Paul to image Israel as the beautiful olive tree into which the wild-olive branches of the Gentiles are grafted. And he has John the Divine envision an entire forest of trees that becomes the wood of life in the heavenly Jerusalem.

Or consider how the Spirit develops the image of the *city* itself. It is buried first in the garden of Eden — in the *paradeisos,* in the hint of the ultimate Central Park that foreshadows what civilization (from *civis,* city) is destined to become. And when the human race fails to build that city properly, God destroys nearly all of it in the Flood and then confuses its tongues at the tower of Babel. But he doesn't despair. He calls Abram to build it in a mystery — on the road, as it were, and in the descendants of a septuagenarian who has no children, and who has to wander as a citizen of nowhere for twenty-five years until his wife bears his firstborn. The Spirit continues that mystery of a city in the cityless by carrying Abraham's seed into slavery in Egypt and then by transporting them to a wilderness for forty more years on the road. Eventually, though, some solid images of the city appear. The Jews take possession of Jerusalem and fall in love with Mount Zion as the joy of the whole earth. And although they lose sight of the city in the Babylonian captivity, the beauty of its image keeps on drawing them. Jesus himself weeps over the city, calling it back to its destiny. He who is the Key to the city dies outside the city. And, leaving behind him only the fingerprints of cross and empty tomb, he sends his church forth from Jerusalem to proclaim the Good News that the building of the city, so long hidden, has finally been accomplished in himself.

Or, next to last, take the image of the *rock*. It's glimpsed in Exodus 17, where Moses brings forth water from the rock. It reappears in Isaiah 51:1: "Look to the rock from which you were hewn, and

15

to the quarry from which you were dug." Paul unearths it again in 1 Corinthians 10:4, and proclaims the Rock in the Wilderness to be the Messiah himself: the *Christos* in the Wilderness before the *Christos* is revealed in Jesus. In Matthew 16:18, Jesus uses it again, calling Simon the son of Jonah "Peter" *(Petros)* and saying, "Upon this rock *[petra]* I will build my church." And in a consummate stroke, Psalm 118 introduces the image of the cornerstone, and Matthew, Mark, and Luke apply it to Jesus as the Stone which the builders rejected — while 1 Peter 2:6-8 declares Jesus a "stone of stumbling and a rock of offense." The rock, therefore, is one of the choicest illustrations of the Spirit's hand in Scripture. Starting with a rock standing alone in a desert, he can lead Isaiah to say the LORD's people were quarried out of a rock that already contained them, Paul to declare that the rock was Christ, the Gospel writers to proclaim the rock as a cornerstone, and Peter to make the cornerstone an image of the scandal of the cross and the paradox of the mystery of Christ.

And last of all, in a masterpiece of multiple image-retrievals, the Spirit reintroduces all the buried icons at once and makes them burst forth like a fountain at the end of Revelation. The City lies foursquare on twelve foundations of precious Stones; it has no need of sun and moon because the Lamb is its Light; the Water reappears as the River of Life to nourish the Tree of Life, whose leaves are for the healing of the nations; and the River flows forever through the New Jerusalem — which is now not only the heavenly City but also the Bride at the eternal Marriage Supper of the Lamb.

I know. If you were trained in Scripture by twentieth-century scholars, you probably find this "image" approach to the Bible boringly antique. But since it has a good two thousand years under its belt — and since the system we've been raised in is lucky if it's had two hundred — take a long, second look at the old way. You may have nothing to lose but your yawns.

❧

Let me now illustrate how the images of Scripture work by going back to your question about eternal punishment. Hell, as everlast-

16

ing separation from the final wedding reception, is clearly present in the Bible, especially in the parables of Jesus. But when Jesus brings up the subject, he does so largely by means of stories, not in terms of propositional theology. He doesn't discuss the doctrine of hell or try to prove that hell exists; rather, he gives word-pictures that show its dynamics in action. Accordingly, if you want to get a handle on what he's saying, you have to look at the details of the imagery he uses, not just jump to the conclusion that he's solving the problems your theology has given you. I've commented extensively on the parables in my earlier books, *The Parables of the Kingdom, The Parables of Grace,* and *The Parables of Judgment;* but I've come up with some new images since then, and I'd like to explore those with you. If I repeat anything I've mentioned before, it's just for the sake of clarity.

The first thing I want you to look at is the fact that almost all of Jesus' parables of judgment (and, in particular, the parables of the Virgins, the Talents, and the Sheep and the Goats) come late in his ministry, just before his death on the cross. Matthew 25, where those three occur, marks the end of the "talk" period of Jesus' earthly career and the beginning of the "final action" phase. (Chapter 26 opens the narration of his passion, death, and resurrection.) It's almost as if Jesus is saying, "I want you to listen closely to what I'm saying. But even if you don't understand a word of it, I'm still going to do what I came to do: draw everyone to myself in my death. You'll see me in the morning when I rise. Now, though, the night is coming."

That brings me to another point about Jesus' parables of judgment. Contrary to the usual opinion that the good go to heaven and the bad go to hell, Jesus sets up his stories so that goodness and badness don't count at all in the final judgment. The only thing judged at the end of these parables is faith, not works. What made the wise virgins wise wasn't that they brought extra oil with them but the simple fact that they didn't leave the party to which the Bridegroom had invited them — that they had faith in his inclusion of them in his wedding. And what got the foolish ones locked out at the end wasn't their failure to bring oil; it was their failure to have the faith to stay at the party and meet him when he came. The shut door at the end of that parable — and the outer darkness for the fellow with one talent, and the departure of the goats into everlasting fire — all turn out to be reaffirmations of the truth that nobody goes to hell in Jesus' parables of judgment except from a heaven they were already in, but for their unbelief.

And therefore the first word over all of us at the Last Judgment will always be a "You're just fine by me" spoken by the Word in the presence of his Father — who in turn will say over each of us, "This is my Son, the Beloved, in whom I am well pleased." If after that we still object to God's insistence on our acceptability, then we can go to hell. But it will be a hell right in the midst of the heaven of all that approval — because "the gifts and the calling of God are without repentance" (Rom. 11:29). Indeed, the hell of it all (for which not one of the Bible's grim depictions is a bit too strong) may well be that God will never stop telling us how wonderful we are, while we won't shut up long enough to trust his judgment.

This eternal tension between faith and unfaith is made crystal clear at the end of the parable of the Prodigal Son in Luke 15. When the father goes out to plead with his older son to join the party of acceptance he's already at, Jesus gives us a new and benevolent image of the seeming standoff between heaven and hell — an image that suggests, to me at least, Jesus' own descent into hell. All the older brother can think of out there in the courtyard is the unreal world of bookkeeping and blame that's ruining his life. He's in hell right at the party: he can't stop griping about his father's neglect or his brother's prodigality — and all that, in spite of the fact that he's been the owner of the whole farm since the beginning of the parable. But the father persists in his good will toward both sons. He doesn't condemn anybody; he simply stands there pleading. In effect, then, what he says to his stubborn son is, "Look, Irving; why don't you just cut the self-pity, go on in, kiss your brother, and have a drink?"

Do you see what Jesus has done? His imagery has put hell inside the party: he uses "presence" imagery for it rather than "separation" imagery; and like a brilliant movie director, he ends the parable with a "freeze-frame" shot of the father and the older brother in the outer courtyard. We never find out whether the father gave up and kicked the grouch out, or whether the grouch stopped grouching and joined the party. What Jesus gives us is a film with an unresolved final scene. The father's last line is, "Son, you are ever with me, and all that I have is yours. It was right that we should make merry and be glad; for this your brother was dead and is alive again, he was lost and is found." My paraphrase for that would be, "As far as I'm concerned, Irving, we're all okay here. Just trust me and enjoy the self you keep losing in your efforts to find yourself." And since that freeze-frame picture has been before our eyes for two thousand years, why can't the image of Jesus' presence to the damned be true forever?

I realize that this image of hell and heaven in the same place may go against the grain of your usual interpretation. (I was once booed at a church gathering for even suggesting it.) But that's not the fault of the parable. It's because of the habit (to be honest, almost everybody's habit) of reading Jesus' parables as if they were bits of advice to us rather than revelations of the mystery by which God embraces us all, no strings attached. If I may repeat myself just a bit, then, the first rule in reading the parables is to begin with the God Characters — and to look at them long enough and hard enough to catch a glimpse of the outrageous, paradoxical God they represent. Read them that way, and you'll find a richness of salvation by grace that you haven't seen before. Read them the other way around, though, and you'll never get off the dime of salvation by your own efforts — of thinking there's something you have to do before grace will actually kick in for you.

But that habit of reading the parables backwards dies equally hard. The literalism that surrounds us has so steeped our minds in the logic of propositional statements that we've lost our ability to hear anything addressed to the logic of the imagination. Consequently, we miss the point of almost everything Jesus has to say — because it's the logic of images that makes his parables tick. He doesn't give them so that the flickering lights of reason will burn brighter in our heads. He tells them to put out all the lights we have so that in the darkening of mere intellect we can see the images of the true Light who, by his incarnate presence, is the Light of every human being. The parables aren't plausible elucidations of things we already know; they're hard sayings, even riddles. After his very

19

first one, the parable of the Sower (Matt. 13:10), his disciples ask him, "Why do you talk to them in riddles *[parabolais]* like that?" And Jesus' answer is, "I speak in dark sayings *[parabolais]* so that seeing they will see and not perceive, and hearing they will hear and not understand" (Matt. 13:13). In short, he tells us parables so we won't catch on — because anything we could catch onto would be the wrong thing.

Only the logic of the imagination can fathom the parables — or the Bible itself, for that matter. Think of it this way. The house of human discourse has many floors; but in our time, we live almost entirely in the basement of propositional logic. Down there, we're surrounded by TV commercials, talk shows, police procedurals, hospital dramas, situation comedies, newspapers, radio, magazines, and Internet chitchat — every one of which inundates us with cellar talk. To be sure, every now and then a novel or a poem may invite us upstairs to experience the sunlight of imagery. But that's too much brightness for us. Soon enough, we run back down to bask under the fifteen-watt bulb of literalism. Imagery isn't just hard for us to look at; the eyes of our minds are blind to it. And as a result, we're blind to Scripture as well because, as I've said, it's the images of Scripture that make it a cohesive whole. The Bible, if you will, lives in the upper rooms of the house of discourse. It has, of course, its propositional moments, its times in the basement of language where it hangs up the socks and underwear of revelation. But its major thread, the grand clothesline on which it displays the principal garments of salvation, lies exclusively in the realm of imagery.

∼

A while back, I said that literalism sees Scripture as a box of particles, all equally true, all propositions of the same sort. Let me give that image a twist now and put it differently. What literalism actually does is turn Scripture into a Coke machine filled with uniform cans of revelation. If you approach it on that basis, all you need is the right change, or better yet the right key, to fetch out the saving soda. But having a key to a revelation machine is not what understanding Scripture is about. There is no key to the Scriptures. You can't unlock it as you would a soft-drink machine and snatch out what you decide you want from it. I've already suggested that it's more like a womb than a soda dispenser, and that you have to wait till it's ready to deliver and not try to force your own schedule on it. Now, however, in ending this chapter, I want to expand on that image to show how it might deal with the problems that literalism has given us.

Think about the womb of a pregnant woman. If you could go inside it any time you liked, you would find not only a fetus but much else besides: placenta, umbilical cord, amniotic fluid, and so on. You could decide (correctly) that all of those things were necessary to the development of the child in the womb. But since you can't just barge inside before the time of delivery, your decision about the ultimate necessity of those things has to wait until then. Only then can you see the distinction between child and placenta clearly enough to decide to keep the child and discard the placenta.

So also with many things in Scripture. Let me give you just a few examples, beginning with one that all Christians are agreed on. During the long gestation of the Word of God Incarnate in the Old Covenant, the sacrificial system of worship (see Exodus and Leviticus) could be seen as necessary to the growth and well-being of the Word — that is, as the placenta of the Word of God Written. But when that Word is actually delivered in the New Covenant — and in particular when the author of the letter to the Hebrews comes along and insists that the ceremonial law of the Old Testament was only a shadow, a prefiguring image of the good things to come, not their ultimate icon *(eikōn)* and sacrament (Heb. 10:1) — blood sacrifice can be seen for what it really was. Its final scriptural function was to serve as a preparatory word-picture or metaphor of the ultimate redemption, not its final revelation.

Do you see what possibilities that opens up with regard to other so-called contradictions? Try this one on for size. The Old Testament condemns usury and permits slavery; but Christians now read Scripture as allowing interest on loans and forbidding the ownership of other human beings. If you take both of those readings as the finally delivered Word of God Written on the subjects in question, you have a problem. But if you view those Old Testament prescriptions as amniotic fluid and the New Testament ones as the child who was in the womb of Scripture all along, you're problem is solved. You discard the former and keep the latter.

Or, to take a harder case, consider another conflict. Both the Old and the New Testaments disapprove (to say the least) of homosexual relationships; but many Christians, myself included, now see that position as untenable in the light of the delivered Word's drawing of all persons to himself. Naturally, if you're locked into reading every scriptural pronouncement as literal truth, you have to condemn same-sex marriages, no matter how committed the partners may be to the Bible's standards of fidelity and charity. But if you can see your first reading as a culturally determined shadow of the way things ought to be (that is, as an umbilical cord which served to nourish the values of marriage back then), and the second reading as the true and final image of how all sexual commitment now stands in the presence of the Word himself as finally revealed, same-sex marriages cease to be a difficulty for you. As I said, that's a harder case. If you're not with me on it, I understand perfectly. Even if we both accept the image of Scripture as the womb of the Word, you're free to say that those disapprovals aren't just an umbilical cord to be disposed of, they're the Word himself speaking. But the image also leaves me free to see things the other way around. The beauty of thinking in images is that we can agree to disagree without having to run each other off the farm.

I leave you to think about that. All I'm suggesting is that if we can break through to the upper floors of discourse where the logic of the imagination plays freely, we may find the air easier to breathe. But since all images break down eventually — and since none of them absolves us from the search for the mystery that lies beneath them — let me set aside the metaphor of the womb for now and give you another image.

TWO

The Juggling Act

My new image for the way in which the Holy Spirit turns the Bible into God's Word Written is the figure of the Juggler. That metaphor occurred to me after reading a piece in the *New Yorker* about Michael Moschen, one of the most spectacular and perhaps most mystical practitioners of the art of juggling. The article, by Mark Levine, began by simply describing Moschen's act: no explanations, no conclusions, just an attempt to convey the audience's bafflement at what he does. Contrary to the impression given by most jugglers, Moschen doesn't come across as making objects submit to his control; instead, he appears to leave them free to be themselves and to enter into a relationship with their essential uncontrollability. Here's Levine's description:

> After the theater darkened, the curtain rose on the juggler's black-clad figure kneeling on a bare stage in a pool of white light. Electronic music twittered . . . the sliver of a crescent moon dangled in the background. The juggler stared at his hands with the intensity of a blood-spattered Macbeth.
>
> Each of Moschen's palms held a glowing, lumpy mass, which he seemed to find both fascinating and repellent. Slowly, he parted his hands, and each mass gained clarity until it became a stack of luminescent balls.
>
> Now the balls began to move, seemingly on their own, crawl-

23

ing over one another, then separating. . . . Moschen watched this activity as if he had just found himself the recipient of an incomprehensible gift. He released the balls, one at a time. They rolled off his fingers with a languid, weighty collapse onto the floor, where they sketched a line between him and the audience. When the juggler leaned toward the balls, the audience leaned, too. Finally, Moschen was left holding a single ball. He rubbed his open palm under the ball, and the ball seemed to float; so did Moschen. Then the ball drifted over his body, gliding along the back of one hand, along an arm, across his chest and neck. The ball was lofted into the air and landed on his forehead, from which it seemed to push him down on the stage. He lay on his back: the ball remained perched on his forehead like an abstract image of a perfectly formed thought. Impishly, the juggler crossed his feet.

You may now have an inkling of how I'm going to use that image as a metaphor for the relationship between the Spirit and the Bible; but to give you a few more hints, let me add three shorter quotes from Moschen:

> Juggling is a right-brain activity that involves letting yourself go, letting things happen. To make three balls go around with two hands is so contrary to reason that it just makes you giggle. It's mystical.
> The most interesting part of my work is learning how to touch an object, and discovering how the objects give up their secrets. What I'm after is the essential spiritual magnetism of a shape.
> I made a rule that I would never close my hand around the ball, that I would always keep my hand open. It's virtually impossible to have real control over an object if you're doing that. It was the most difficult choice I could make, because it's the opposite of what a juggler is supposed to do. It offers only vulnerability.

Levine goes on to say, "Moschen told me that this technique taught him that juggling could be less about control than about the

24

struggle to accept the fear and turmoil surrounding uncontrollable events." Finally, Levine also includes this comment by the magician Ricky Jay. He called Moschen "the greatest conceptual juggler of all time," but declined to elaborate. "What I say to my friends is, 'Go and see this man.' And when they ask what he does, I say, 'Just go.'"

The main reason why it pleases me to see the Spirit as that kind of Juggler is the way it improves on the images I've used so far for his inspiration of Scripture. Not only does it get us away from the image of a controller; it liberates us from the bad habit of viewing the Bible as a container for the Word of God. That, I think, was the hitch in my attempt to portray it as a matrix. While the image of a womb was better than the image of a boxful of truth particles or a Coke machine holding cans of salvation-soda, it was still a picture of something wrapped around the Word. Like all such figures, it failed to do justice to the Reformation's sweeping insistence that the Scriptures *are* the Word of God. That statement, you see, is the highest of all possible views. It goes even farther than calling the Blessed Virgin the mother of God. While we do indeed hold that the Person in Mary's womb is none other than the Word of God in human flesh, we never say that Mary herself is the Word. She may be a living rather than an inanimate vessel for the Word; but she's still a container, not the Word himself in Person.

Accordingly, if you view Scripture as one long performance by a Divine Juggler who's bent on revealing the Word himself, you finally escape from the blind alley of trying to discover the Word by sifting through the details of the Bible's contents. When you watch a juggler, you clearly see all the balls, hats, cigar boxes, or canes he's dealing with. But you can appreciate the significance of what he's doing only by looking at his act as a whole. It's the mystery of the entire performance that astonishes you, not the incidental properties of the items he's juggling.

And mystery is precisely what literalism misses. Let me make something clear, however: I don't see literalism as the exclusive property of the religious right. To me, liberals are just as guilty of it as conservatives. Their attempt to cull out of the Bible a more dependable Jesus than the less-than-historical one they think they find on its pages is only a liberal version of the fundamentalist view.

Both see Jesus' words as more central to his redemption than his Person. Both seem to think that we're saved by what he said or did, when in truth we're saved by Who He Is — by the Person of the Word of God Incarnate.

Take the Jesus Seminar, for example. What they're trying to do is decide which of Jesus' words should be called his "actual" sayings and which should be demoted to some lesser status; but they're still looking for something they can call literally true. In the light of the Moschen imagery, however, their efforts amount to little more than rummaging through the details of the Spirit's biblical juggling act and deciding that it's only the round balls and not the square boxes or odd-shaped hats of Scripture which reveal what he was doing. They're still looking for a key that will admit them to the "original" historical text. But that's a wild goose chase: the canon of Scripture as it stands is the only such text — and it's certainly the only one we hold in common. For better or worse, the only Jesus anywhere in history is the Jesus of the historical New Testament. Any other is just an educated guess.

Indeed, the Jesus Seminar's device of color-coding the words of Jesus in descending order of authenticity makes the same mistake that the old red-letter editions of the New Testament did. The implication in those was that his words deserved red ink because they were somehow more significant than anything else about him — that the Sermon on the Mount, for instance, should get more attention than his death on the cross or the mystery of a new creation revealed in his resurrection. But that runs clean contrary to the faith of the church — as at least some of the members of the Seminar clearly recognize (Marcus Borg, to name one). The apostolic preaching in the book of Acts, for example, gives us almost nothing of what Jesus said in the Gospels; instead, it contents itself with proclaiming his identity as Lord and Messiah, and buttressing that announcement with quotations from the Old Testament. To this day, in fact, we still don't profess our faith in the things he said, or even in the transactional efficacy of the deeds he performed. When we say the Creeds, we put our trust in the Person he is: that is, in Jesus himself, the eternally begotten Son who is God from God, Light from Light, true God from true God, of one being with the Father — and who is the Word by whom all things are both made and redeemed. Therefore it's *Who He Is,* not just stuff he says or does, that redeems the world.

But back to the Spirit's juggling act. A juggler can even make a mistake during his performance (drop a ball, fail to keep a hat in the rotation) and still captivate us by his strange dialogue with uncontrollability. Consider one more passage from Levine's article:

> Moschen said, "A juggler is not a secure person. A juggler, by definition, should be an insecure person." The exhilaration of a breathtaking performance can be shattered in an instant by the dreaded "drop." Moschen, who tends to acknowledge the occasional drop by gazing querulously at the wayward ball, claims not to be averse to being exposed as mortal. "If you want to get anywhere you have to embrace failure, not flee from it," he said.

Do you see what that allows you to say about the Spirit's "failures" in Scripture? Is the Bible's apparent date of 4,004 B.C. for the creation of the world a problem for you in view of the astrophysicists' contention that it happened billions of years ago? Does the Spirit's inclusion of factual errors give you pause? (The hare does *not* chew the cud, despite Leviticus 11:6.) Are you upset by the early church's expectations that the second coming of Christ was just around the corner? Don't let such things bother you. Don't let them take your eye off the mysterious revelation that's at the heart of the Spirit's whole juggling act. They aren't problems to be solved; they're simply wayward cigar boxes that got out of the Spirit's hand at one point. They're failures that he embraces — that he gazes at just as querulously as we do — without letting them stand in the way of getting on with his astonishing performance. When the Spirit inspires the Bible, he doesn't operate as a puppeteer, controlling its authors and editors and readers like so many marionettes. He deals with whatever is available to him. He gets his way by embracing their intractability, not by overriding it.

That was the trouble with the old "verbal dictation" theory of biblical inspiration. The image of a secretary slavishly transcribing the words of an infallible executive left you no choice but to stop in your tracks at every contradiction and prove that an obvious mistake wasn't the boss's fault after all. Think, for example, of all the breath that's been wasted trying to harmonize the six-day biblical account of creation with the paleontological evidence of evolution. Think of the folly which held that the Bible's account is the only historically correct one and that God poked the fossil remains into the layers of the earth just to test your faith. But if you're willing to see the Bible as the juggling act of the Spirit, the six-day account in Genesis becomes not an instance of faulty control over the details of revelation but a marvelous ball with a mind of its own — a ball that can still be used as an image even if it turns out to be questionable as a scientific description. Its literal inaccuracy becomes just a bit of fallibility during a total performance in which the *mystery* of creation and redemption is infallibly revealed.

It's the whole performance of Scripture, therefore, that's the communication; the literal significance, or even the eternal truthfulness of every single part, is not necessarily the point. The rule for dealing with the Bible is the same as the rule for watching Moschen juggle: Don't sit around asking questions; "just go" — just let the entire act take you in. You're in the hands of a Juggler who's even better than Moschen.

∼

Time now for a more detailed example of what I mean by "letting the entire act take you in." In the previous chapter, I mentioned the system of animal sacrifice in the Old Testament and the letter to the Hebrews in the New. I want to spend the rest of this chapter examining both of those — and some of the other "dropped balls" they involved — as integral parts of the Spirit's juggling of Scripture.

There's no question, at least among Christians, that the passion, death, and resurrection of Jesus are the crucial events in the biblical revelation. For one thing, the amount of space allotted to those mysteries is remarkable. No other week in Jesus' life gets anything like the attention given to Holy Week and Easter: eight out of twenty-eight chapters in Matthew, six out of sixteen in Mark, six out of twenty-four in Luke, and a whopping ten out of twenty-one in

John. All four Gospels, therefore, are deliberately structured as a drama that has its climax in the cross and the empty tomb.

For another thing, as the Spirit juggles the balls he's already picked up in the Old Covenant, the entire history of Israel becomes a series of prophecies (indeed, *sacraments*) of the Incarnate Word's death and resurrection. In fact, the early church "proved" the centrality of those mysteries by pointing out that they had been in the scriptural works all along. Jesus, they maintained, died and rose "in accordance with the Scriptures" meaning the Hebrew Bible, and in particular its translation into the Greek of the Septuagint version.

For example. In the book of Acts (4:27, 30), Jesus is referred to as the *pais,* the "boy" or the "child" or the "servant" of God. At first sight, this seems an odd locution — almost a mistake, or a least a strange substitute for the more usual title, "Son *[huios]* of God." But it isn't a mistake; it's the Spirit's juggling. In the Greek (LXX) version of the book of Isaiah, the word *pais* is the ordinary translation of the Hebrew word *'ebed,* "servant," in the so-called Servant Poems. (See, for example, Isaiah 42:1.) So in calling Jesus the *pais* of God, the early church was in effect "proving" that those poems were actually anticipations (or again, even sacraments) of the real presence of Jesus himself as the Suffering Servant in the passion of his people Israel — in short, that they were fingerprints of God.

In all likelihood, of course, the original writers of such passages probably didn't have a clue that God's promised Messiah would suffer and die. To include such a wayward ball in God's redeeming scenario was inconceivable to them. In their eyes, the Lord's Anointed had to be a winner. And since the idea of a Messiah who would die as a criminal under the curse of God's law was unacceptable to them, most of the passages they provided as props for the Spirit to juggle portrayed the Messiah as a conquering hero who would make Israel the world's undisputed superpower. Still, as is obvious in the "suffering servant of Yahweh" passages in Isaiah, the Spirit did manage to put sufficient mystery into his juggling of the messianic ball to leave open the possibility of seeing those passages as images of Jesus' passion and death.

But, for the third and most important thing, the Spirit felt free to gaze at that wayward ball long enough to find another way of picking it up and getting it back into the act. That's where animal sacrifice and the letter to the Hebrews come in.

To the eyes of faith, the cross and the resurrection can indeed be seen as signs and sacraments of the world's redemption. But to the eyes of the mind, they're simply unreadable as saving acts. Intellectually speaking, the cross is a sign written in black ink on black paper: to the eye of history, it proclaims nothing but the death of a malefactor. The cross's prominence in Christian churches is based on the church's paradoxical belief that the Person who died on it is God himself, not on any value the cross might have as a "religious" symbol. And Jesus' resurrection is just as unreadable by the intellect as his cross. The only difference is that it's a sign written in white ink on white paper: all the mind has to go on are disputable reports of an empty tomb and ambiguous appearances by the risen Jesus. None of the resurrection's historical details proves a thing about forgiveness or the new creation — or even about the resurrection of a single other person. Once again, only faith can see any significance in it. But faith can never be trust in the transactions of a religion; it can only be trust in a Person who, thanks to no religious acts at all, is the One we believe him to be.

But, even worse for the mind, neither of those two mysteries made the slightest change in the course of day-to-day events. After the crucifixion, sinners went right on sinning, warriors continued to war, torturers still tortured, and liars kept on with their favorite indoor sport: the world persisted in being the graceless mess it always had been. Nor did the resurrection visibly accomplish what faith says it does. Far from showing us a creation manifestly made new, it left behind it the same old creation as before. All anyone can see in its aftermath is the universal death that still claims everybody, the pervasive sin that still gums up the works, and the torrent of tears that flows uninterrupted from human eyes. The mystery remains a mystery. It remains hidden from every faculty but faith.

That, you see, was the problem that confronted the Spirit when the author of Hebrews sat down to write. What the presiding Juggler needed was some image of reconciliation, some way of gazing at those unreadable signs to reveal the mystery they were really about. So what he got the writer to come up with was the entire sacrificial system of the Old Testament — and in particular, the images of victim, blood, death, and priesthood. Here's how it worked. Jesus bled and died on the cross, just as any victim would have. But if the Spirit could take the imagery of blood sacrifice in the Tabernacle and Temple and shine it on the cross, the problem was solved. Those sacrifices could be seen as preliminary (though in themselves ineffective) prefigurings of a mystery that could now, in Jesus, be seen by faith. They could be called (as Hebrews 10:1 calls them) shadows cast upon former days by a Substance who was clearly revealed only in future times. Their significance, in other words, lay not in the transactions they prescribed but in the Word who anticipated himself in them.

Plainly, the Spirit and the author of Hebrews had hit a mother lode. Not only did the butcher-shop atmosphere of the Old Covenant sacrifices make the barbarity of the cross readable as forgiveness of sins; it opened up a host of new images as well. Under the old system, the priest and the victim were separate beings, one acting, the other acted upon. Now those images could be applied to a single Person: Jesus was both priest and victim, agent and patient, rolled into one. Better yet, while the blood of the victims offered by the high priest didn't accomplish what it promised, the blood of Jesus did. The high priest had to repeat the same sacrifices year after year — as if their effect had worn off with the passage of time. But Christ, having appeared as "a high priest of the good things that have come . . . entered once for all into the Holy Place, not with the blood of goats and calves, but with his own blood, thus obtaining eternal redemption" (Heb. 9:11-12). Better still, the wayward ball of animal sacrifice became, under the Spirit's querulous gaze, something that could be seen as an integral part of his whole performance: he made it a permanent — even a pre-eminent — feature of his act.

But best of all, this imagery enabled the Spirit to incorporate into the letter to the Hebrews not only Paul's insight that the ceremonial law couldn't save but also John's insistence that the Person who saves the world in Jesus is none other than God himself Incarnate. At last, he'd found somebody who could say that the death and resurrection of Jesus were not transactions but mysteries — not a new religion, or even a religion at all, but a New Covenant with the whole human race. "Religious" acts invariably cause us to image God as someone who stands at a distance from the human race, and who insists that he won't bridge the gap until we make some appropriate effort to close it from our side. Unless we make effective sacrifices, or believe the right doctrines, or behave in the proper way, God just won't budge. But Hebrews, right at its beginning, takes us clean away from all such religiosity: "By many steps [polymerōs] and in many images [polytropōs] God long ago spoke to our ancestors by the prophets; but in these last days he has spoken to us in [his] Son, whom he appointed heir of all things, through whom he also created the worlds. He [the Son] is the radiance [apaugasma] of God's glory and the exact image [charactēr] of God's very being, and he sustains all things by the word of his power" (Heb. 1:1-3).

All in all, this device of seeing the death of Jesus as a more perfect sacrifice made by the Son as both priest and victim was, and still is, a brilliant performance. But alas, it wasn't the last of the problematic balls or errant cigar boxes the Spirit has had to deal with. His juggling can't be confined to just the production of the Bible; it must also take into account the ongoing use of the Scriptures in the life of the church. As I said, the Bible is not a manual intended to provide individual readers with correct answers to questions about religion, ethics, or theology. In every age, it's the living voice of the Word himself in dialogue with the church. And because the church's responses to his speaking continually produce new drops and fumbles, there will always be the possibility that the Spirit will have to work them too into his juggling.

Which brings me to what happened to the image of the cross as a sacrifice during the Middle Ages and in the aftermath of the Reformation. Over that longish period, the notion of Jesus' death as an atonement for sin came to overshadow the mystery of Incarnation by which he draws all things to himself. What he did at one particular point in time preoccupied Christians more than Who He Is at every point from the very beginning. And that led directly to a profound mistake. After the Reformers had talked long enough and loud enough about the sacrifice of Christ as the single operative device in redemption, they gradually forgot that the device started out in Hebrews as an image for the mystery of Who the Word is. They turned his sacrifice into a literal transaction that fulfilled an external requirement with which he was bound to comply. They began to image the things he did (his dying, his rising, his ascending) as a series of tests he had to pass in order to become the Savior of the world. In short, they gave the impression that Jesus was the Savior because he got 1600 on the Salvation Aptitude Test.

No doubt that image strikes you as even more far-fetched than my image of the Juggler; but they actually came up with a number of variations on it. Here are just three. Some of them maintained that his perfect score on the cosmic SAT was achieved by paying a ransom to the devil who had kidnapped the human race. Others held that he achieved top rank in the celestial mathematics portion of the test because he alone could calculate the magnitude of the satisfaction owed to his offended Father. Still others insisted that he qualified for the Harvard of heaven because only he aced the verbal part by giving flawless ethical prescriptions. But in every case, it was the test he passed, not the Person he is, that did the trick.

None of that will wash, however. If you want to use the school image at all, you have to say that Jesus gets his *summa cum laude* degree as Savior by influence alone — by the sheer pull he has with his Father — not by dint of his achievements. He goes to the head of the class because he's the Headmaster's only Son, not because he does the right stuff. To think otherwise is to imagine that on the refrigerator in the heavenly Father's kitchen there was a Post-it note that read, "Reminder: look for somebody who can pass the sacrifice test; otherwise, the world will be out of luck."

It was Duns Scotus, I believe, who almost alone among medieval theologians pointed out that the Father could have accepted any offering Jesus made and still have considered him the Redeemer of the world. If I may take that insight a step further, it seems to me that the Father could have accepted anything whatsoever that Jesus did — up to and including his doing nothing but inhaling and exhaling without lifting a finger or saying a word — and still have been just as happy with him. His just hanging out in the world (which is pretty much what the New Testament says Jesus did for the first thirty years of his life on earth) would have been quite enough to enable the Father to proclaim, as he did at Jesus' baptism, "This is my beloved Son, in whom I am well pleased." Jesus doesn't *become* the Savior at some late stage of his career; he already *is* the Savior at every moment of his life. He's the incarnate Lord when he lies in the manger as a baby. He's the Messiah of both Jew and Gentile in his circumcision. He's the Word of God when he asks a twelve-year-old's questions of the rabbis in the Temple. He's the One by whom all things are made when he putters in Joseph's carpenter shop at thirteen. And he's the Way, the Truth, the Life, and the Resurrection before, during, and after his parables, his healings, his passion, his death, and his resurrection.

Admittedly, Scotus never went quite that far. Nor did another of my favorites, Athanasius (of whom more later). He, right along with most of the ancient fathers, took a dim view of people who suggested that the Word Incarnate might have done better to avoid the shameful and public death of the cross. In fairness to myself, though, I would point out that they were simply defending the "proof value" of such a death. Dying in a corner somewhere, Athanasius felt, would have left too many questions about the reality of Jesus' death, not to mention the factuality of his resurrection. What I've been championing is the more central truth that the Word who draws all to himself is present not only in Jesus' death but in every death throughout the world. I've been trying to show that the cosmic effectiveness of Jesus' acts depends only on the Word who indwells them, not on their circumstances or their instrumental value. Whatever Jesus does, the Word does; and likewise, whatever the Word does, Jesus can be said to do as well.

Though that may strike you as odd, it's nothing more than a restatement of the classic Christian doctrine that goes by the name of *communicatio idiomatum,* "the communication of idioms" — and which posits an *interpenetration* of the *properties* of both Christ's divine and human natures *in one Person,* in the one Word of God who acts in each nature. It holds that as long as you're talking about the Person of Christ, you may apply any idiom or property of either nature to him. For example, it's legitimate to say that "the carpenter of Nazareth made the world," since the Person who labored alongside Joseph in the shop was the Word by whom all things are made; and it's equally proper to say that "God died on the cross," because the

Person who underwent a human death in Jesus was likewise that same Word. Obviously, a human carpenter couldn't have made the world, and God as such can't die; but the same Person could and did do both jobs. Those two statements may be extravagances; but they're based on the even greater extravagance of a God who becomes flesh.

My point is that Jesus was never cramming to save the world or working his way toward a redemptive performance that lay in his future. True enough, the stages of his life and ministry are a progressive revelation and realization of Who He Is; but at no point does he *achieve* the status of Savior. Once again, he doesn't insert salvation into a world that didn't previously have it. From his conception to his ascension — in fact, from the foundation of the world to its consummation — the redeemed world that God loves has always been the renewed creation which the Father sees and cherishes in his only begotten Son.

~

But back to the Reformers. To be sure, there was a skin of reason on their insistence that Jesus' death on the cross was a single oblation once offered and that it constituted a "full, perfect, and sufficient sacrifice, oblation, and satisfaction for the sins of the whole world." Medieval theologians had long since fallen into the trap of portraying the church as an agency rather than a sacrament — a kind of public utility that hooked people up to Jesus one customer at a time rather than a witness to the mystery of a hookup already accomplished for all time in the Word Incarnate. They'd given the impression that Baptism, for example, was necessary because without it there couldn't be hope for anyone. In their hands, the sacrament of Baptism became a piecework insertion of grace, an immunizing shot of forgiveness for persons who would otherwise die of their sins, or even the issuance of an insurance policy against the fires of hell. And they did much the same thing with the Eucharist. They downplayed the Mass as a sacrament of the all-sufficient sacrifice of Christ for everybody and turned it into an actual repetition of that sacrifice to be applied as the church saw fit to needy cases. The net effect was that, like the sacrifices of the Old Covenant, the "sacrifices of masses" had to be reapplied whenever new problems came along (new sins, perhaps, or new people who needed to be speeded through purgatory). But the most dangerous implication of such imagery was that the grace of God in Christ was an iffy piece of business — just one more bait-and-switch offer from an airline that advertised a bargain fare to heaven and then, when you tried to book the flight, told you there was a surcharge. Which, if it's not exactly what Luther said about the theology he grew up with, is pretty much how he felt about where it left him.

It was against ecclesiastical marketing strategies of this sort that the Reformers set Scripture's clear insistence (especially in Hebrews) on the sole and complete efficacy of the sacrifice of Jesus once offered on the cross. They said that he, not the church as a go-between, was the only Mediator and Advocate. And they maintained that the only possible response to that gracious proclamation was faith, not the fulfillment of ecclesiastical requirements or the performance of individual good works. Everything that needed doing had been done by him; there was nothing left for anyone else to do except trust him. However, in handing the Spirit those renewed, "once for all" images of sacrifice, mediation, and faith, they failed to spot a certain waywardness in them that the Divine Juggler would have to cope with in his ongoing performance.

Take sacrifice first. When we think of the work of the Reformers, we generally imagine them as doing a total overhaul of the Middle Ages' thinking. But in fact that's not the case. While it's true that they did correct many unscriptural assertions by medieval theologians, there were still a fair number of things they didn't reform. They (along with their Renaissance compatriots in the sixteenth century) may have been the first harbingers of modern times; but they were not themselves "modern" people, at least not as that word is used now.

The word *modern*, by the way, has an interesting history. At the time of the Reformation, it simply meant "present-day" as opposed to "in the past"; it had none of the progressive, forward-looking overtones it later acquired. In fact, for both the Reformers and their Renaissance counterparts, the "modern" thing to do — the main thrust of their immediate preoccupation — was to look back to antiquity. The Reformers leapfrogged over the Latin of the Vulgate and returned to the original Hebrew and Greek of the Scriptures; the Renaissance types took classical — not medieval — Latin as their guide to suitable style. In fact, it wasn't until the seventeenth century that "modern" began to have its current force; and it wasn't until the eighteenth and nineteenth centuries that it took on the evolutionary, "new is better" connotations it now has. So the truth is that the Reformers were all late medievalists: even when they did try to reform the Middle Ages' misrepresentations of the sacrifice of Christ, they hardly noticed that they were leaving unreformed the exaltation of Atonement over Incarnation, which they inherited as part of their medieval formation.

True enough, almost all of them accepted the Incarnation of the Word as a major article of faith. Still, their habit of imaging the Atonement as a transactional sacrifice continued to infect the rest of their theology. They went right on seeing the Incarnation as an afterthought — as the late arrival of a divine serviceman to customers who could have used him earlier, rather than as the mystery of the Word who'd been present in all his creatures from the foundation of the world. Even when they did admit that the Incarnation applied to the whole human race, they still didn't break the medieval habit of seeing it as a deal contingent on individual compliance rather than as a gift already given to everyone.

Which brings up the matter of faith. To be sure, the early Reformers rightly insisted that God saves the world by grace and that the only response grace calls for is faith. Salvation, they said, comes *sola gratia* (by grace alone), and it can be apprehended *sola fide* (by faith alone). But even if most of them avoided turning faith into a quasi-work, their successors fell into that very trap. Right up to the present day, many Protestants see faith as an instrument by which persons who don't have salvation will be able to get it. They imagine themselves (as the medievalists imagined the church) as having some agency, some necessary role in their redemption. Not only are they still stuck with the image of a Savior who had to take a Salvation Aptitude Test; they see themselves as having to pass a faith exam.

But that's not what either the Bible or the Protestant tradition says. As I've already pointed out, the great insight of Scripture and the Reformation is that the world goes home to the Father by pull alone — by the Father's delight in a beloved Son who draws all to himself in his death. But that truth has been eased into oblivion by the image of a job that won't get done unless we give it a helping hand. Redemption really does end up looking like the box of chocolates I foisted on the Spirit in the prologue to this book. Everyone already has the gift; all anyone can do is trust it or not trust it. The abiding presence of the gift doesn't depend on anybody's faith; it depends only on the Giver — on the Lamb of God who takes away the sins of the world, not just the sins of the cooperative. Accordingly, faith doesn't *do* anything; it simply enables believers to enjoy what Jesus has already done for them.

Among all the Reformers, only Calvin got this right — and he got it right only half the time. When he taught that salvation is unlosable by the saved (his doctrine of the "final perseverance of the elect"), he said that nothing they might do or fail to do had any bearing on the triumph of Christ in their lives. Grace did it all. Neither their good works, nor their sins, nor even their faith or unfaith had any effect on their eternal bliss. But when he fell back into the medieval habit of fussing over the fate of the damned, he slipped. While he didn't exactly make hell the result of human actions, he maintained that the damned were predestined to it by the inscrutable will of God. In short, he did manage to keep grace graceful — but only at the price of making God himself ungracious.

Finally, though, take the Reformers' stress on Jesus as the Mediator *(mesitēs)* between God and the human race. The word *mesitēs* occurs only five times in the New Testament. The two appearances in Paul's letter to the Galatians (3:19-20) refer not to Jesus but to the rabbinical tradition which held that the law was given by the "hand of a mediator" (that is, by angelic go-betweens — by other agents than the one God). In this passage Paul is contrasting that notion with the fact that when God saves the world in the Person of Christ, he does the job himself, through no intermediary at all. *Mesitēs* is also used in 1 Timothy 2:5: "there is one mediator between God and man"; but the verse goes on to identify that mediator as "the *man*

Christ Jesus," thus holding up Jesus' humanity as the mediatorial aspect of his being and leaving his Divinity to be expounded in other passages. (See, for example, John 1:1, where he is called the "Word [who] was God," and Titus 2:11-13, where he is said to be "our great God and Savior, Jesus Christ"). Thus as God the Word, Jesus stands as the great Non-Mediator who saves us in Person. Finally, the two occurrences of *mesitēs* in Hebrews (8:6 and 9:15) mention Jesus as the mediator of a "better covenant" and a "new covenant"; but they make that claim on the basis of the promise of God in the Person of Christ and not on the kind of transactional mediation portrayed in the Old Covenant.

There's no question, of course, that Jesus' actions in his *human* nature are mediatorial: as the Gospel of John points out, "no one has seen God at any time; it is the only begotten Son, who is in the bosom of the Father, who has declared him" (1:18). But what John has in mind is a Son who is of one being with the Father, not a Son who is essentially other than he is. Accordingly, Jesus is and is not a mediator. He is, because his humanity functions as a go-between — we would never have heard the Good News except from human lips, or read it except in writings from human hands. But he's not, because in his Divinity he's God himself. And therefore if we forget that he's simply one Person, our preoccupation with his easily grasped human status as mediator inevitably tempts us to write off his divine non-mediation as too paradoxical to be believed.

Which, sadly, is where the minds of too many Christians have come to rest. They can accept the images of Jesus as teacher, wonderworker, good example, intermediary, and general-purpose Mr. Niceguy; but when they do that, the image of Jesus as God in Person simply vanishes from their minds. One of the stubborn facts about the logic of images is that just as bad money drives out good, so plausible images drive out paradoxical ones. Or, to change the metaphor, unhitching an image like mediation from the mystery of the Incarnate Word who's actually towing it has the same effect as unhitching a trailer and turning it into a home on cement blocks. The intellectual trailer park you've decided to live in can't get you anywhere; and the only Tractor who can put you on the road to your true Home escapes your mind completely. And since that's pretty much the predicament of what passes for a good deal of theological thinking these days, I think it's time to set aside the image of the juggling act and take a closer look at where the brighter side of the logic of images can take us.

Welcome to the world of re-hitched trailers.

THREE

Escape from the Trailer Park

The first trailer I want to re-hitch to the tractor of Incarnation is the venerable but generally neglected image (from the letter to the Ephesians) of the *recapitulation* of all things in Christ. In Ephesians, Paul (or a very bright disciple of his who had a knack for living in Paul's head) speaks of the redemption of the world not as the removal of great chunks of its history or the pruning out of its sins but as the recapitulation, the retelling of all its stories, good and bad, in the Person of Jesus the Incarnate Word. First, though, let me give you a little background on the letter itself.

Most biblical scholars have doubts about Paul's authorship of Ephesians, and a good many have similar questions about Colossians. The reasoning behind these opinions can be found in any good commentary and need not be dwelt on here. But almost everybody admits that both letters are deeply "Pauline" — that is, logical developments of the authentic theology of Paul. Even if they were written by someone else, that disciple was brilliant enough to take his master's thought where Paul himself might have gone if he had lived long enough to wrestle with the vocabulary of late first-century Gnosticism and use it in the service of his earlier insights. In any case, very few good theologians in the history of the church have balked at including both Ephesians and Colossians in their attempts to elucidate the implications of Paul's teaching.

Now for the passage in Ephesians (1:3-10) that leads up to the

41

image of recapitulation (the *italicized* words are the phrases to which I'm going to pay particular attention):

> [3]Blessed be the God and Father of our Lord Jesus Christ [I'm going to translate "Christ" [*Christos*] as "the Messiah" throughout this passage; my reason will become clear in the next chapter] who has blessed us with every spiritual blessing in the heavenly places *in the Messiah,* [4]just as he chose us *in him* to be holy and blameless before him in love *before the foundation of the world.* [5]He destined [*proorisas*] us for adoption as sons [*huiothesian*] through Jesus the Messiah, according to the good pleasure of his will, [6]to the praise of his glorious *grace* [*charitos*] that he freely bestowed on us *in the Beloved.* [7]*In him* we have redemption through his blood, the forgiveness of our trespasses, according to the richness of his *grace* [8]that he lavished [*echaritōsen*] on us. With all wisdom and insight [9]he has made known to us the *mystery* [*mysterion*] of his will, according to his good pleasure that he set forth *in the Messiah* [10]as a dispensation for the fulfillment of times [that is, of all history], to *recapitulate* [*anakephalaiōsasthai*] all things *in him,* things in the heavenly places and things on the earth.

Now for the image of recapitulation. Suppose that you and I are reading the same novel and that as we discuss it, we find we have different views of what the author has in mind. You read it as a story filled with immoralities that the author will have to get out of the narrative if she's to avoid a tragic ending for her characters; I read it as moving toward a happy conclusion even if those imperfections remain in the story to the (non-bitter) end. What do I do to convince you that my reading is the better one? I recapitulate the story for you. I retell it, going over all the rough places and showing you how the author's later developments make them smooth without once mitigating their roughness. I recount for you everything you've added up as disaster and present you with a new total that adds up to triumph. In other words, I go over the same ground we've both covered in the book, but I re-speak it all in the light of its reconciling ending.

As a matter of fact, an author will often recapitulate parts of her own novel in the process of telling its story. She may have confronted you early on with the nastiness of a particular character; but later, in a flashback, she'll recount that character's faults and invest them with a plot-advancing significance they didn't have at the time. (This is what the Holy Spirit was doing when he got Paul, in Galatians 4, to retell the story of Sarah's meanness in forcing Abraham to cast out Hagar, the mother of his son Ishmael, and recount it as an image of the relationship between grace and law.) Or she may take a previous image and recast it as a device for displaying the true character of her story's hero (which is what the author of Hebrews did in chapter 7 when he took the mysterious figure of the king-priest Melchizedek in Genesis 14 and re-imaged him as an antitype, a prefiguring of Christ as the great King and High Priest). Or she may even create an image out of something that in itself was simply a piece of factual bad news and use it to gather up into one all the lesser images of good news she's already tucked into her story (which, of course, is what the Spirit did throughout the New Testament when he took the bare fact of Jesus' execution on the cross and made it comprise such disparate images as the trees in Eden, the blood of the Paschal Lamb, the water from the Rock in the Wilderness, and the sacrificial victims of Old Testament worship).

But note well what this device of recapitulation does not do. It doesn't go back over the story and simply remove events or people who no longer square with where the author now wants to go with her plot. She doesn't change what's already happened: only an inept writer solves the problems of her characters by running a bus over them or by proving that their sins never happened. And only a foolish reader tries to understand a book by ignoring the things he can't make sense of. For both author and reader, the inconveniences of the story must remain inconveniences to the end. If they're to be seen as not counting in the last analysis, it must be not because they're discounted but because they're recounted in such a way that their tragedies, without ceasing to be tragic, are converted into amazing grace.

That, I think, is what the author of Ephesians had in mind when he introduced the image of recapitulation. He knew that given the Bible's frequent excoriation of bad behavior in general and of sins in particular, it would be all too easy for readers to conclude that God has no use for sinners and will deprive them of the grace of a happy ending. But that conclusion runs clean contrary to the overarching thrust of Scripture. In Romans 5:8, we're told that Christ died for us "while we were still sinners," not after we'd gotten our acts straightened up. And in 2 Corinthians 5:21, we find the alarming declaration that Jesus, who knew no sin, "became sin for us." The Bible, when all is said and done, does not inform us that God walks away from sinners. It shows him going after the lost sheep until he finds it (Luke 15:4), running to prodigals and kissing them before, not after, they make their confessions (Luke 15:20), and staying with the woman taken in adultery until all her accusers have gone away in shame (John 8:9).

In other words, the God of Scripture spends his time in history wading chin-deep with us through the mud of our sins. But as he re-tells the story of our journey in the Godhead — as the eternal Son whispers it into the ear of the Father in the bed of the unity of the Spirit — he re-speaks our sins as *all right* in his Trinitarian pillow talk. We go to our final home with our sins, not without them, for the simple reason that every moment of our history is held in him. If that home is heaven, we'll get there because our sins are held as no problem in his gracious recounting of them, not because we've gotten rid of them. And if that home happens to be hell, it will be not because we've failed to get our sins out of our history but because we've refused to trust his recounting of them and insisted on trusting only our old way of adding them up. Both heaven and hell, you see, are populated only and entirely by forgiven sinners. The difference between those two conditions is faith or unfaith in Christ's recapitulation of all things — in the forgiveness of the Lamb of God who takes away the sins of the whole world.

❧

To make this clearer, I'm going to give you a few more paragraphs on Jesus' parables — this time as exercises in recapitulation.

I've been ordained fifty years now; but it wasn't until recently that I noticed something peculiar in the parable of the Lost Sheep

(Luke 15:11-17). The shepherd doesn't go back to the ninety-nine when he finds the stray one; he goes straight home and throws a party. That changed my interpretation of the entire story. Jesus wasn't saying that the ninety-nine represent the good people of the world and the one represents the sinners. (The ninety-nine "just persons who need no repentance" whom Jesus mentions at the end of the parable weren't people he thought well of; he introduced them as a dig at the self-righteousness of the Pharisees he was rebuking.) So he wasn't dividing the world into two camps; he was making each camp stand for everybody: the unlost ninety-nine were the world as it thinks it is, and the lost one was the world as it really is. It was the shepherd's passion to find the lost — the shepherd's own losing — that drove the parable, not the ethical acceptability or unacceptability of his flock. Lostness — even the sinful lostness of tax collectors and prostitutes — was just his cup of tea.

That led me to another insight. When I saw that Jesus had presented me with two opposed groups as a way of talking about everyone, I realized he was making use of a figure of speech called *hendiadys* — a way of speaking that deals with *one thing by means of two*. "Good and faithful servant" was the first illustration that occurred to me: it simply meant "very faithful servant," not "ethical and religious servant" — just as "good and tired" means that I'm ready for bed, not that I'm sinless on the one hand and exhausted on the other. After that, I decided to try applying *hendiadys* to Jesus' depictions of contrasting sets of characters in many of his parables. The five wise bridesmaids, for instance, weren't the good girls of the story, nor were the five foolish ones the bad girls. (As a matter of fact, Jesus portrays the wise ones as nasty pieces of work and the foolish ones as innocent victims of their selfishness.) The real point of the parable wasn't the tension between good and evil but the tension between faith and unfaith. To say it once again, the only thing the wise ones did right was to trust the Bridegroom's inclusion of them and not leave the party; and the only thing the fools did wrong was to distrust him and look for an open hardware store at midnight.

Once more, the starring role in the parables belongs to the "God Character," not to the "human race" characters. Jesus' stories are intended to show us first of all how God in Christ operates in the world, not how we ought to behave. Unless, for example, our primary focus in the parable of the Sower is more on his haphazard sowing of the seed than on the various types of ground he sows, we'll miss Jesus' message. So too with other parables. Unless we pay more attention to the father than to the prodigal or his resentful brother, we'll miss his meaning in that one as well.

Unfortunately, though, that's what we almost always do. In fact, it's our preoccupation with the supporting cast that's led us to misname so many of Jesus' most important stories. The parable of the Lost Coin should be called The Party of the Woman Who Lost One Coin; the Laborers in the Vineyard should be The Party of the Beneficent Vineyard Owner; the Ten Virgins should be The Party of the Late (or perhaps even the Absent) Bridegroom; and the Prodigal Son should be The Party of the Father Who Lost Two Sons. In every one of those parables, you see, it's the mysterious behavior of the Christ figure, not the plausible actions of the human figures, that drives the story. In short, it's a God Character who goes out of the "god business" on whom Jesus wants us to fix our minds — because the Christ on the cross in whom we believe did exactly that. At three o'clock on a Friday afternoon, he tore up the "God Union" card we tried to give him and insisted on working without one.

We're almost ready for the parable of the Father Who Lost Two Sons as an image of recapitulation. But first, let me show you how the image of recapitulation sheds new light on another easily misread passage of Scripture. In the sixth chapter of the letter to the Romans, Paul writes,

> [11]So you also must consider yourselves [*logizesthe,* "account yourselves," or perhaps even "recount yourselves"] as dead to sin and alive to God in Christ Jesus. [12]Therefore, do not let *sin* exercise dominion in your mortal bodies, to make you obey its desires. [13]Nor should you present your members to *sin* as weapons of wickedness, but present yourselves to God as those who are alive from the dead and present your members as weapons of righteousness [*dikaiosynē*] for God. [14]For *sin* will have no dominion over you, since you are not under law but under grace.

If we read that passage simply as a warning to avoid sins, I think we miss the mark Paul was aiming for. We put ourselves right back in the old bind of living under law instead of grace. We turn it into exactly the kind of veiled threat I once suggested the father might have given to the prodigal after he made his confession the second time: "You're home, dear boy; but watch your step." We're so in the habit of imagining that God won't think kindly of us unless we get rid of our vices that the idea of God's accepting us right in the midst of them seems just plain un-Godly. But it's just that kind of un-Godliness that God in Christ reveals to us on the cross. He goes out of the god business we've been wishing on him ever since Adam and Eve, and he drops dead to the subject of sin. His death doesn't tell us we have to be sinless before he'll be nice to us; it invites us to trust the Incarnate Word who's made our sins of no account in himself. It proclaims that their presence in our lives doesn't stand between him and us anymore.

That, I think, is why Paul so often talks about sin in the singular rather than in the plural. "Sins" is a word too easily equated with wrong actions, with bad behavior we think God can't or won't deal with. So when Paul speaks of *sin,* it seems to me (as it apparently did to the writer of Ephesians) that he's best understood if we read him as referring to our way of telling the story of our lives as opposed to God's way of retelling it. He's talking about trust in Christ's recapitulation of us, not about our own reformation of our sad histories. "All that is not of faith is sin," Paul says in Romans 14:23. For him, the opposite of sin is not virtue but trusting God instead of ourselves — which is the same point that the Bible makes in the story of the Fall in Genesis 3. The sin of Adam and Eve was not that they committed some specific wrong; it was that they stopped having faith in God's hands-off way of retelling the tale of good and evil and trusted only their own hands-on scheme for making themselves gods — their efforts to control the good and abolish the evil by their own devices. They would make themselves righteous, and they would force everybody else to toe the same line. But that's not the righteousness Paul was referring to in the passage I just gave you above. What he had in mind was not some hard-earned uprightness of our own. He was thinking of the righteousness of Christ, which is a gift already given to everybody through the irremovable presence of the Incarnate Word by whom all things are made and restored.

All of this is neatly summed up in the final words of the passage from 2 Corinthians 5:21 that I've quoted several times now: "[God] made him who knew no sin to become sin on our behalf so that we might become the righteousness of God *in him.*" That, incidentally, is why I italicized all the references to *in the Messiah* and *in him* in the Ephesians passage at the beginning of this chapter. It's the mystery of Christ's presence in all of history — and above all, the mystery of the presence of all sinful history in him — that saves the world. It's not that the Word shows up late in history and waves a magic wand that gets rid of people's sins. It's that he's always had the whole, lost world in his arms, and that in his recapitulation, its lostness becomes just another occasion for celebration. Which, nicely enough, brings us back to the father and his two boys as an image of recapitulation.

Both the prodigal and his older brother are clearly shown as telling their own version of their history. The younger one, feeding pigs at the trough in the far country, sees his life so far as a disaster and concocts a plan of his own to straighten up the mess: he'll go home and ask to be made a hired hand. And the older one, standing in the courtyard at the end of the parable, portrays his whole life as nothing but a history of abuses suffered and grudges held. But the father, at every point in the parable, has always held both their stories as he's retold them in and to himself. He kisses the prodigal before the boy gets a word out of his mouth; and he goes out to plead endlessly with the older brother (even though he doesn't seem to listen) to trust that he's retold his story as well. All you have to do is remember that the father is an image of the Word Incarnate — another fingerprint of the Divine Suspect — and the whole parable lights up. It's exactly what Ephesians 1:10 was talking about: the recapitulation of all things in Christ, things in the heavenly places and things on earth.

See what happens when you get the trailers of imagery re-hitched to the Tractor of the Word? The cart is no longer before the Horse, and the ride turns into a trip instead of a dead end.

FOUR

A Visit to the Ballpark

As a matter of fact, the contest over whether the cart or the Horse should be in first place has been the church's favorite sport for two thousand years. So let me switch gears yet again and give you another metaphor: the imagery of *baseball* — and in particular, some images of the first few pitchers on the mound in the church's oldest ball-game.

Some of those pitchers (Peter, for instance) threw well enough in the early innings, getting Jesus way out in front of opposing batters (old-line Jewish hitters, for example, who wanted the Gentiles to submit to circumcision and the dietary laws). But as the game wore on, Peter tended to lose his control — so much so that the Divine Manager (the Spirit) had to go to the bullpen for the greatest middle reliever of all time, the Apostle Paul. Even he, however, wasn't quite up to the task: he was hit by a line drive from the Emperor Nero in the year 64 and had to retire from the game. The Manager was forced to bring in his star closers (the writers of Colossians and Ephesians and the author of the Gospel according to John) to protect the lead Paul had run up. All in all, the Holy Spirit (then and since) has had some iffy ball-games on his hands. Whenever a pitcher managed to get Who Jesus Is ahead of what the opposition thought he said or did, they came up with new batters who weren't fazed by the old fastballs and sliders.

But enough of the sports metaphor for the moment. T. S. Eliot

49

summed up the situation far more elegantly in one of his *Four Quartets:*

> . . . And what there is to conquer
> By strength and submission, has already been discovered
> Once or twice, or several times, by men whom one cannot hope
> To emulate — but there is no competition —
> There is only the fight to recover what has been lost
> And found and lost again and again: and now, under conditions
> That seem unpropitious. But perhaps neither gain nor loss.
> For us, there is only the trying. The rest is not our business.
>
> (*East Coker,* V)

Now for the analysis of the games, beginning with the earliest pitch, Peter's sermon on the day of Pentecost (excerpts from Acts 2:14-36):

> [14b]Men of Judaea [*andres Ioudaioi*] and all who are dwelling in Jerusalem, let this be known among you, and listen to my words. . . . [22]Fellow Israelites [*andres Israēlitai*], . . . Jesus the Nazarene, a man attested to you by God with deeds of power, wonders, and signs that God did through him among you (as you yourselves know) — [23]this man, handed over to you by the determined plan and foreknowledge of God, you crucified and killed by the hands of those outside the law. [24]But God raised him up, having loosed the pains of death because it was impossible for him to be held in its power. . . . [36]Therefore let the entire house of Israel know with certainty that God has made him both Lord and Messiah, this Jesus whom you crucified.

The first thing to note about this earliest example of the apostolic preaching is its radical Jewishness. Peter wasn't proclaiming a "Christian" religion, or even a religion at all. He was announcing the fulfillment in Jesus of the whole history of Israel. His audience that day consisted entirely of Jews; all his fellow witnesses to the resurrection were Jews; the crowd at Pentecost were either Jews or Gentile converts to Judaism — and of course Jesus himself was a Jew. Furthermore, in identifying Jesus as Lord *(Kyrios)* and Messiah *(Christos)*, Peter was putting the Horse squarely before the cart. He wasn't trying to say what Jesus had taught or how the things he did effected God's plan. He was proclaiming, in strictly Jewish terms, Who Jesus Is.

Consider Peter's use of the term *Kyrios*. I'm going to try and make the case that in the year 29, that was as close as early first-century Jews could come to expressing the Divinity of Jesus. For them, calling Jesus "God" was simply an impossibility: it would have blown all the circuits in their monotheistic minds. The Second Commandment, as they understood it, forbade all images of God. Nothing that even looked like a created thing, not even the human Jesus, could be given such a title. But *Kyrios* was the Greek word that the Septuagint (LXX) translators (all Jews) had used to represent the Name of God (the tetragrammaton, *YHWH*) whenever it occurred in the sacred text. (By Jewish custom, this Name was never pronounced when the text was read; instead, in deference to the Third Commandment, they substituted the word *Adonai*, "Lord." This substitution was automatic: it was rather like what might have happened if Christians had decided that the Name of Jesus was too holy to say out loud and had taken to reading it as "our Lord" every time it occurred in the New Testament.) In any case, *Kyrios* from the mouth of Peter definitely carried with it, for readers familiar with the LXX, a strong connection with the sacred Name, and therefore with a Person who would eventually be identified as God.

This may seem like a bit of a stretch, since I can't prove that Peter was familiar with the LXX (or could even read Greek). But it's important to remember that Luke (or whoever may have been the author of Acts) actually wrote these words not in the first third of the first century but in the last third. Furthermore, it's quite clear that as early as Paul, and even in other New Testament writings (Luke, Colossians, Ephesians), the Hebrew Scriptures were regularly quoted from the Septuagint. Indeed, the lengthy Old Testament passages I omitted (". . .") from Peter's sermon come from the LXX text of Joel 3:1-5 (in our Bibles, Joel 2:28-32) and from the words attributed to David in Psalm 16:8-11. Accordingly, it seems to me that the application of the title *Kyrios* to Jesus by the early church carried the same freight of Divinity it had in the LXX.

Which brings us to *Christos, Messiah,* Christ. Both *Messiah* in Hebrew and *Christos* in Greek come from the verb "to anoint": the Messiah, the Christ, is the Anointed One (*Mashiach*) of God, just as his ancestor David had been (and just as Israel itself is in Psalm 105:15 and Habakkuk 3:13 and even as the Persian king Cyrus is in Isaiah 45:1). Therefore, I don't think it's a good idea to use the English word "Christ" when translating the early church's references to Jesus as *Christos.* They're far too Hebraic to be expressed by an English word that now has unmistakably Christian overtones. To our ears, "Christ" leads us to forget the radical Jewishness of the early church's preaching and to assume a "Christianity" that simply wasn't there yet. Furthermore, it tempts us to compound the felony by assuming (all Paul's labors to the contrary) that Judaism and Christianity are on opposite sides of an impenetrable fence. True enough, by the end of the first century some of the later books of the New Testament displayed the beginnings of such a standoff — and by the middle of the second century, the divorce between the two had degenerated into the anti-Semitism that has plagued the church ever since. But it wasn't there at the start; it wasn't there in Paul; it wasn't there in Colossians and Ephesians — and despite all the scholars who have found the Gospel of John anti-Jewish, I don't think it's there, either.

Accordingly, I'm all in favor of translating *Christos* as "Messiah" in all of those writers (especially John) as often as possible. As a matter of fact, it seems to me that when John does apply *Christos* to Jesus (far less often than the other Gospel writers do), he almost always uses it in the sense of *Messiah,* even though by John's time (very late first century, if not early second), the "Christian" connotations of *Christos* had taken up permanent residence in most people's minds. It's almost as if he was trying to make the same correction I have in mind: "No matter what you may think," he seems to be saying, "*Christos* means *Messiah.*" Interestingly, John is the only one among all the New Testament writers who uses the Greek transliteration of *Messiah,* which is *Messias:* he puts it into the mouths of people who were using the Aramaic form of the Hebrew word (the disciple Andrew in 1:41 and the Samaritan woman at the well in 4:25). And in both instances, he identifies it with the Greek word *Christos.*

But back to Peter as the first pitcher. In proclaiming Jesus as Lord and Messiah, he runs up an impressive score. He sets Who Jesus Is dramatically in front of all other considerations. But then he (and the early Jerusalem church right along with him) begins to falter. His early throws bore amazing fruit: three thousand converts (all Jews) were baptized after his sermon at Pentecost; five thousand believers (likewise Jews) were added after the healing of the lame man in Acts 3. But that very success now started to cause trouble: Gentiles as well as Jews began to be attracted to the fellowship of faith in Jesus the Messiah. As I said, at first most of these seem to have been Greek-speaking converts to Judaism; but they too soon became problems. The "Hellenists" in the Jerusalem church began to complain against the "Hebrews" because their widows were being neglected in the daily table-serving that was a feature of the church's common meals.

This sounds to me like what I've had to listen to for fifty years in parish churches on the eastern end of Long Island: the "summer people" bellyaching because the "locals" treat them as outsiders, as second-class citizens. And sure enough, in Acts 6 the Apostles do what any concerned and politically adroit pastor nowadays would do: they appoint a committee. They invite the church to select seven reputable men whom they can put in charge of the problem so they can devote themselves to more important things. Not surprisingly, all seven turn out to have Greek names (don't tell me there wasn't any politics in the early church), and the Apostles arrange a special ordination service for them. The men, of course, were the first Deacons of the church; but whatever peace was made by this solemn laying on of hands was short-lived. As the influx of Gentiles continued, it began to bring in plain, uncircumcised types who had never even thought about keeping the Jewish law. So, as a result, the Jerusalem believers began to do what T. S. Eliot says the church has done ever since: to lose what it had just so brilliantly found. It was the church's first flirtation with the dangerous game of putting the cart before the Horse.

Here's how it worked. Since all the first believers in Jesus were

Jews who kept the entire Mosaic law (ritual and dietary commandments included), the Jerusalem Apostles decided that Gentile converts could not become official boy-scout believers until they kept
either the whole of that law or at least those parts of it that would
give them a reasonable facsimile of Jewishness. In other words, having gotten the Horse of Who Jesus Is (in the Jewish terms of *Kyrios*
and *Christos*) before all else, they proceeded to park the cart of ritual
Jewishness in front of Gentiles who were already believers in Jesus as
Lord and Messiah. Once again, they acted like parish pastors. But
this time their instincts for parochial crisis-management led them
to welsh on the catholicity of their original insight. In Acts 15, they
prescribed a modified adherence to the law for the converts whom
Paul had brought in through his mission to the Gentiles.

As that chapter was written by Luke, this strategy is presented as
a brilliant compromise: James and the rest of the Jerusalem leader-
ship drop their insistence that the Gentile converts be circumcised,
but they give themselves the sop of still requiring observance of certain aspects of the dietary and moral laws. In Acts, Paul is depicted
as going along with this "solution." But if you look at what Paul
himself says in Galatians, a different picture emerges. In that letter,
he's adamantly opposed to the Jerusalem church's meddling in the
Galatian believers' affairs. (In 2:8-10, in fact, he contradicts Luke
and says that the only thing James and company ever told him was
that he should "remember the poor.") Moreover, he's furious with
what he calls Peter's hypocritical behavior. Before the Jerusalem
deputation arrived in Galatia, Peter sat at the same table with
Gentiles; but after they showed up, he "separated himself," for fear
of the "circumcision party."

❧

That gets us slightly ahead of the story, though. Since we've already
begun to deal with the Apostle to the Gentiles, it's time we returned
to the image of the ball game for a more careful look at this second
and perhaps most talented pitcher of all.

In Galatians, and above all in Romans, Paul resoundingly puts
Who Jesus Is in front of anything that made religious requirements

more important than the Person of the Messiah himself. But sadly, the church has time and again put the cart back in front of the Horse. Paul's pitches for the primacy of grace over law, while brilliant enough to foil hitters who look for the law ball, haven't been as successful against batters who can hit endless fouls off the ball of grace. Grace has always been easy to turn into law — and right from the start, Paul has been hard to understand. The biblical scholar Adolph von Harnack once said, "No one in the second century understood Paul except Marcion — and he *mis*understood him." B. W. Bacon later corrected that to "No one understood Paul except John — and he did *not* misunderstand him." Admittedly, John isn't any easier to grasp than Paul; both had complex and subtle minds. But taken together, they go a long way to illuminate each other's murky places.

Even to this day, grace remains hard to swallow. Religiosity and moralism go down easier than free forgiveness. Salvation by our own works sells better than the outrageous "acceptance in the Beloved" that lets disreputable types in for nothing but faith in the Beloved. The human race, faced with the choice between a gift and a deal, will almost invariably prefer the deal. With all its difficulties, though, Paul's pitch for the centrality of Jesus himself as the Messiah, and for the primacy of grace over law, has hung over the outside corner of the plate, tempting many to read it as if it were a law thrown at them, but still keeping its spin as the indisputable ball of grace. And all the reformers who followed him — from John, to Luther, to you or me (with luck) — have never done better than when they followed his example.

Between reformers, however, the church routinely lapses back, often with a little help from its misreading of Paul himself. In his letters, he spends a fair amount of time enjoining upright behavior on the churches to which he writes — so much so that if people want to argue with his radical championing of grace, they can always manage to interpret his moral exhortations as requirements for salvation. Strictly speaking, that's not fair to Paul: he never seriously reneges on grace. But for minds in love with moralism, there's always a temptation to ask questions like these: "But what about all Paul's words in favor of 'living honorably' and against 'reveling and drunkenness, debauchery and licentiousness, quarreling and jealousy'? Don't those urgings mean that we have to behave properly in order to be saved? Aren't we ourselves the ones responsible for 'putting on the Lord Jesus the Messiah' and for 'not making provision for the flesh, to gratify its desires?' [Rom. 13:13-14]. In short, isn't our righteousness a precondition of our acceptance?"

The only honest answer I can give to such questions is to admit that Paul speaks out of both sides of his mouth. From one side, he gives them a very loud "No!": human works simply don't count in God's reckoning. But from the other, we hear the lingering echo of a "Yes!" The No rings out in the long, careful developments of his teaching on grace in the early parts of his letters (for example, in Romans 1-11 and in Galatians 1-4); but the Yes hovers over the later sections in which he gives pastoral advice to his readers (Romans 12-16; Galatians 5-6). In other words, when he's working on the theology of grace, he's quite clear that God has made the Messiah alone the basis for the world's redemption; but when he addresses his Gentile converts, the ethical rigor of his Pharisaic background begins to leak into his letters. When he's confronted with the grosser excesses of Greek behavior (as he is, say, in 1 Corinthians 5:1-13), he reacts to them like the respectable Jewish uncle he never ceased to be: all he can think of saying is "In the Name of God, cut that out!" Still, his Yes to good behavior was always predicated on his prior No to any notion that we're saved by our own goodness. What saves us is only and always the Messiah's righteousness already present in us by grace. Let me quote 2 Corinthians 5:17-21 for you again:

> 17So if anyone is in the Messiah [*Christos*], he is a new creation: the old things have passed away and new things have happened; 18and all things [*ta panta*] are from the God who reconciled us to himself through the Messiah and has given us the ministry of reconciliation; 19that is, that God was in the Messiah reconciling the world to himself, not counting their trespasses against them, and entrusting to us the word of reconciliation. 20So we are ambassadors for the Messiah, since God is making his appeal through us; we entreat you on behalf of the Messiah, be recon-

ciled to God. [21]For our sake he made him who knew no sin to be sin for us, in order that we might become the righteousness of God in him.

It's possible, of course, to misread that pitch. If you come to it thinking that your reconciliation to God is something you have to accomplish for yourself before God will accept you, you'll skip over all the mysterious assertions in verses 17-19 (namely, that it's the gift of a new creation given by God in the Messiah), and you'll go straight to the last "be reconciled" in verse 20 and read it as a command to get yourself reconciled. But if you read it with a mind open to what Paul has already said, it's quite plain that he's talking about a reconciliation that's already been accomplished for the whole world by God in Jesus — that all the old things (the disaster that creation has made of itself) are things of the past, and that the new things (the reconciled wonders of the new creation) are accomplished facts for everybody. It's also clear that the ministry of reconciliation which God has entrusted to the church can't possibly mean that the church is an agency whose job is to offer the possibility of reconciliation to a world that doesn't yet have it. Once again, what God has given the church is simply the word of a reconciliation completed: the Good News that in the *Christos,* the whole creation has been put to rights from square one. The church, Paul says, is precisely a peaceable ambassador inviting trust (faith) in a treaty that's already been put into effect by God, not a warmongering general threatening "No treaty until you lay down your arms!"

Nevertheless, because Paul didn't distance himself as much as he might have from the church-as-field-marshall imagery, it was left to others after him to bring out more clearly the imagery of reconciliation as a mystery revealed in the Messiah — as a free dispensation long hidden in the world but now finally shown forth in Jesus, not a proffer of good will conditional upon human responses.

～

That note of mystery brings us to the rest of the star pitchers in the church's earliest ball-game: the authors of Colossians, Ephesians, and John. Previously I mentioned some of the questions that scholars have had about Colossians and Ephesians. The old tradition, of course, held that Paul was the author of both; but now almost no one thinks he wrote Ephesians (or that it was written to Ephesus, or even that it's a letter at all). In the earliest and best manuscripts, the single reference to Ephesus in verse 1 is omitted; and the contents of the letter are so generally applicable that some scholars have suggested that it should be considered a "catholic epistle" — or even that it was meant to be the preface to a collection of Paul's authentic letters. As for Colossians, most are agreed that its heavy borrowing from the Gnostic vocabulary puts it too late to be included among Paul's authentic letters.

While that's all persuasive enough to lead me to share those views, let me play my cards face up here and tell you why I don't think any of it matters much in the larger context of Pauline theology. To do that, I want to make a point about Scripture and the imagery of baseball that I've been using in this chapter.

The Bible is not a collection of essays by independent theologians; it's one long, theological ball-game. True enough, the successive pitchers (the Old Testament Prophets, Jesus, Peter, Paul, the writers of Colossians, Ephesians, and John's Gospel) were talented participants in the game — and each of them deserves the closest attention to what he himself said. There's nothing wrong with taking them one by one and trying to discover the historical Jesus, or the real meaning of Paul, or the essence of John. But from the point of view of the Manager of the team, none of that is as central to the outcome of the game as his own management: his bringing Paul in to rescue Jesus from Peter and the Jerusalem church; his calling of Mark, Luke, and Matthew from the bullpen to supply what Paul omitted; and his use of the authors of Colossians, Ephesians, and John to finish what Paul started. In short, you have to read the New Testament as a team performance. The tag line to remember here is "The Gospels were written for the sake of the [Pauline] Epistles." The game's final score can't be known until all the players have had their innings. All of the Gospel-writing (possibly even in Mark and certainly in Luke, Matthew, and John) has to be dated after Paul's death in 64: those books are commentary on Paul, not prefaces to his work. And in the case of John, his Gospel comes so late that it can be read as the last word on nearly all of the New Testament.

As I read Colossians and Ephesians, they depict a struggle between two different ways of looking at Jesus. The first (which I've already noted) is to see him as the insertion of the Incarnate Word into the world at a given time and place — and then to see the subsequent benefits of that insertion as a series of transactions arranged for by the church. This does have a certain plausibility: Jesus was born, lived, died, rose, and ascended in specific historical circumstances; and at times the church has indeed given the impression that it was a franchisee charged with marketing his salvation to an unsaved world. But if you simply let it go at that, you find yourself faced with questions. For one thing, what about all the people who lived and died before Jesus showed up? Are Adam and Eve saved? Are Cain and Abel? For another, what about those who died after Jesus but before the church got to them? Did Alaskan residents born in 100 A.D. have the benefits of his death and resurrection? If so, on what basis? If not, how is that fair? And for a third, were the Gentiles outside Jesus until they did something to get themselves in? Are the unbaptized within Jesus or just out in the cold?

The church has certainly wrestled with such questions; but its answers to them have often made more problems than they solved. Generally speaking, they've been based either on legal fictions like the "imputation" of Jesus' righteousness to those beyond his reach in time and space, or on theological jury-rigging that equates people's "natural" goodness with an unknowing acceptance of Jesus himself. In any case, they all fall short of stating what the church presumably believes — namely, that in Jesus' death, the whole world's sins are taken away, and that in his resurrection, everybody rises. In a nutshell, the answers beg the questions by overlooking the New Testament's frequent insistence on a "new creation" *(kainē ktisis)* in *Christos*.

To cure that habit, we have to go to the other way of looking at Jesus — the way championed by Colossians and Ephesians. Instead of seeing the Incarnate Word as inserted into history, these writers stand the picture on its head and show us all of history as drawn into the Incarnate Word from the foundation of the world. For them, the Word is like a Divine Magnet, and his sinful creatures are like particles of iron filings carelessly flung down on the paper of the world. They lie wherever their fallen natures compel them to; but when the Magnet comes down and dwells under the surface of the paper, they're rearranged: they're repolarized into the order the Magnet has always willed for them. The Word doesn't manhandle them back into line or change their essential nature; he acts mysteriously — simultaneously close up and yet at a respectful distance. So too with the authors of Colossians and Ephesians. They take Paul's words "in the Messiah" and "in him," and they present them to us as images of a mystery that lies beneath the surface of all being. Here's a sampling.

First, from Colossians. Whether this letter was written by Paul or not, it explicates and extends his insights to their logical conclusion. The reason why Paul so fiercely opposed circumcision for Gentile converts is simple: in his view they didn't need it because in the Messiah they were already Jews — already the Chosen People, the Israel of God — without lifting a finger or undergoing any subsequent operation. Look at Colossians 1:13, for example:

> [13]He [God] has rescued us from the power of darkness and transferred us into the kingdom of his beloved Son, [14]in whom we have redemption, the forgiveness of sins. [15]He is the image [*eikōn*] of the invisible God, the firstborn of all creation, [16]because in him all things in heaven and on earth were created . . . all things were created by him and for him, [17]and he himself is before all things, and in him all things consist [*synestēken*, "stand together," "hold together"].

This so obviously proclaims all of history in the Messiah rather than a Messiah poked into history that it needs almost no comment other than to go directly to the passage in which our author decides to take the Gnostic term *mystery* and make it the centerpiece of his argument for the cosmic *Christos*, Colossians 1:24-27:

> [24]Now I rejoice in my sufferings for *you* all [remember, he's writing to Gentiles], and I fill up in my flesh what is lacking in the

Messiah's afflictions for the sake of his body, that is, the church. [25]I became its servant according to God's dispensation [*oikonomia*] that was given to me for you, to make the word of God fully known, [26]the *mystery* that has been hidden from ages and generations but has now been revealed to his saints. [27]To them God chose to make known the glorious richness of this *mystery*, which is the *Messiah in you*, the hope of glory. [Note well: this doesn't say that what has been revealed in Jesus is a job in the process of being done; it presents its Gentile readers with the accomplished fact that they were insiders before they even realized they were outsiders.]

Colossians presses this Gnostic imagery still further into the service of the Jewish Messiah in chapter 2. The danger of Gnosticism to the early church was its tendency to turn Jesus into a mere avatar of the principalities and powers (the "angelic" beings who ruled the universe) and to deny that he was the Word of God himself made flesh. But what was good about Gnosticism (or at least, what the writer of Colossians saw as susceptible of being put to good use) was precisely that same universal quality. The problem of the early church was that it too easily mired itself in this-worldly arrangements for getting people into Jesus or Jesus into people. Accordingly, our author decided that if Gnostic terms could help the church do an end run around such transactionalism by reversing the imagery and concentrating on a mystery that already had the whole world in the Messiah, then why not give it a try? Which is just what he does in Colossians 2. In verse 2, he flatly identifies the Messiah with the mystery, saying that he wants his Gentile readers to be "encouraged and united in love, so that they may . . . have the knowledge of the mystery of God, that is, *Christos*." And a little later, he continues along that line:

[10]and you have come to fullness in him, who is the head [*kephalē*] of every principality and power; [11]in him you also have [already] been circumcised with a circumcision not made with hands [*acheiropoiētos*] in the putting off of the body of the flesh, in the circumcision of the Messiah.

This is remarkable. It's the cosmic *Christos* brought all the way down to something that happened to Jesus at eight days of age; and it's the human Jesus lifted up as the head over all the Gnostic spiritualities in the heavenly places. The events of Jesus' life, without ceasing to be the specific events they were in his earthly career, now become revelations (fingerprints!) of the universal dispensation by which the Catholic Mystery himself dwells among us. Because he is the eternal Beloved — the Icon of God, the One by whom all things are made and in whom all things consist — what happens to him happens to everybody, and what happens to everybody happens in him. His birth in the manger is in all births, and all births are in that manger with him. The deaths of the Holocaust were in his tomb, and his burial was in all the death camps. The whole Gentile world becomes Jewish in his circumcision. The entire creation rises in his resurrection. And transactionalism, at last, is one dead duck.

Do you see what a difference that makes for the church's view of itself? We're not a delivery service hired to take Jesus to the heathen but a witness to the *Christos* already in them. We don't celebrate the Eucharist inside our church buildings in order to find a Jesus who isn't present elsewhere; we receive Jesus in the sacrament of his brokenness so that we can recognize his presence in the brokenness of the world outside. When we take Communion to the sick, we're not bringing Jesus to people from whom he was missing; we're celebrating with them the Incarnate Word they never lost. We are baptized not so that we can possess a Jesus we lacked, but in order that what we already are in him can be declared over us in the waters of the font. And above all, we don't try to live holy and blameless lives in order to keep from getting in dutch with God; we choose that way of life because his holiness and blamelessness have been ours all along, and we've decided to trust his plans for our season more than our own. To say it again: we do it all out of gratitude to the Horse who's already giving us a free ride, not because we're required to by the specifications of some cart we've put in front of him. On to Ephesians.

The author of this treatise was yet another of the great closers in the Manager's bullpen. Even though his pitching (as you'll see in the next chapter) didn't prevent later hitters from getting home runs off some of his wilder throws, he still saved Paul's winning lead. Herewith, a few samples of his best work.

Back at the beginning of my previous chapter, I quoted Ephesians 1:3-10 for you. I won't repeat what I said about it there, but I will make a couple of additional points. First, whoever wrote this passage was obviously familiar with Colossians, and, like the author of that letter, he too was an undisputed master of the mystery hidden in the Messiah. He was also the one New Testament writer who was able to throw the fastball of recapitulation. In fact, he threw it so well that while many of the church's subsequent hitters have taken a swing at it, only Irenaeus, in the second century, really connected with it. But second, I want you to note this writer's peculiar use of the plural pronouns "we" *(hēmeis)* and "you" *(hymeis),* in all their case forms. He alternates carefully between them. He employs "we" when he's referring to the Jews who first received the promise of the Messiah — or to Paul, when he's using the "editorial we" and writing in his name. But when he's speaking specifically to his Gentile readers, he uses "you." Finally, though, he uses "we" again when he's talking about the status of Jews and Greeks alike — both of whom he considers to be "all one" in the Messiah. Watch.

At the beginning of Ephesians 1, "we" is used in the first sense, meaning "we Jews." And it ends, after the 10th verse on *recapitulation,* with this statement: "[11]in whom [in the Messiah] *we* also obtained *our* inheritance, having been destined [*prooristhentes,* "predestined" — one of the pitches that would later make trouble] according to the purpose of him who accomplishes all things according to the counsel of his will, [12]so that *we* [we Jews], who were the first to hope in the Messiah, might be for the praise of his glory." But then the writer shifts abruptly to "you": "[13]In him *you* [Gentiles] also, when *you* had heard the word of truth, the gospel of *your* salvation, and had believed in him, [*you*] were sealed with the promised Holy Spirit." Finally, however, in the next verse, he shifts to "we" in the joint sense of "both Jews and Gentiles": "[14][and that Holy Spirit] is the pledge of *our* inheritance toward redemption as God's own possession, to the praise of his glory." (To see this alternation more clearly, read the first three chapters of Ephesians — in the Greek, they're all a single, run-on sentence — noting each use of "we" or "you" and deciding the various senses for yourself as you go along. It will be a revelation.)

Now for a few additional comments. In Ephesians 2, the author has returned his attention to the Gentiles:

> 2:1*You* were dead in the trespasses and sins 2in which you once lived, following the course of this world, following the ruler of the power of the air, the spirit that is now at work among those who are disobedient, 3among whom all of us [Jews and Gentiles alike] lived in the passions of our flesh, following the desires of the flesh and senses, and *we* were by nature children of wrath, like everyone else. 4But God, who is rich in mercy, out of the great love with which he loved us 5even when we were dead in trespasses, made us alive together in *Christos* — by grace you have been saved — 6and he raised us up together, and sat us down together in the heavenly places in *Christos* Jesus, 7so that in the ages to come he might show the surpassing richness of his grace by kindness toward us in *Christos* Jesus. 8For by grace you have been saved through *faith;* and this is not your own doing, it is the gift [*dōron*] of God, 9not the result of works, so that no one may boast. 10For we are his handiwork, created in *Christos* Jesus for good works, which God prepared beforehand [*proētoimasen:* another easy pitch to hit foul] to be our way of life, so that we might walk in them.

What our author has done here is to take one of Paul's greatest insights and give it cosmic dimensions. In Romans 5:8, Paul had written, "But God proves his love for us in that, while we were still sinners, *Christos* died for us." Now, in Ephesians, that passing reference to the Messiah's embrace of the world *in* its sins (not *after* it gets rid of them) becomes a hymn to the completed work of the Messiah acting quite on his own. And the hymn is about our joy, because we were saved by grace, even when we were dead in our trespasses. We've always been alive together with him; we've always been raised together with him; and we're already sitting in the heavenly places with him now — all because in every now, we've always been in the Messiah Jesus. We're not there because we managed to reform our lives and make ourselves deserving of such a privilege; we're there because it's all his doing: we're his handiwork, not our own. And last but best, we've never been anywhere else; because, as the writer of Ephesians said at the very beginning in 1:3-5: "The God and Father of our Lord Jesus *Christos* chose us *in him* before the foundation of the world." Even before we were born — even when we were nothing whatsoever — we were home in him forever.

Moreover, contrary to much of the church's preaching for two thousand years, neither Ephesians nor Paul seriously means to say that we *will be* made alive after the second nothingness of either our death in sin or our actual, physical death. They insist that we've been alive in him all along, no matter what. Death is not a prelude to our life; it's the very sacrament, the real presence of the life of Jesus in us. Death is the Messiah's chosen place for his eternal rendezvous with us, not a disaster he has to overcome. Everything can go wrong for us; but he never fails to show up for his assignation. In the words of the Lady Julian of Norwich, the great English mystic, "Sin is behovely [sin does indeed fit into the picture], but all shall be well, and all shall be well, and all manner of thing shall be well." Our life in Jesus is a grace irrevocably given and a gift fully received by all. Like it or not, respond to it or not, believe it or not, everybody has it, and nobody will ever lose it.

But in verse 5 of chapter 2, Ephesians carries Paul still further. In saying that God "made us alive" and "raised us up" in *Christos* Jesus, its author uses Greek verbs which are "past" in form but which signify an action that is true for all time. Their import (as I've just said) is not that we're going to enjoy those gifts at some unknown point in the future; they state flatly that we have them now: we *are* alive; we *are* risen. (To its credit, the church has generally gotten this right, at least in its baptismal formularies. Take the Book of Common Prayer, for example. In its rite of Baptism, it states, "In it [Baptism] we are buried [that is, dead as doornails, right now] with Christ in his death. By it, we [now] share in his resurrection [we *are* raised, not *will be* raised].") But those very present truths have completely escaped the minds of most Christians. Try to set them forth in a sermon and the congregation will look at you with wrinkled brows. And if you present them with the third verb (in verse 6), they'll simply write you off as a lunatic.

That verb, you may recall, is *synekathisen* ["he *has sat us together* in the heavenly places in *Christos* Jesus"]. Not only does this say that his life is in our life now and that his resurrection is in our death now; it says that the final destiny of the world in the Messiah is ours now as well. We're not on our way to heaven; we're already there. And since the Messiah is the *eikōn* of the invisible God (indeed, since in John he's God the Word by whom all things are made), the world has never been seated anywhere but *in* eternal life. The deepest truth of our being is that we're *in him:* in the Messiah in whom all things consist and in the Word who became flesh to reveal that eternal truth to us. And if I may throw one last pitch of my own: Even if we end up in hell, we'll still be in him — because even if hell is the literally dreadful place the Bible describes, the only "place" it can exist at all is inside the One who gives it being. There's no escaping the Love that will not let you go.

If you find that outlandish, or even heretical, I understand your feelings. But I can't see how you can justify them on the basis of Paul, Colossians, Ephesians, and company. However, if you simply find it too mysterious, I think I can help you: it's precisely the mystery of the Messiah *(to mystērion tou Christou)* toward which Ephesians has been heading. Admittedly, Paul himself used the word in six places; but only in one of them (1 Cor. 2:1) does he give it anything like the force it later acquired when Ephesians and Colossians came to his rescue and took *mystērion* all the way upstairs. (I've written a whole book on the subject, entitled *The Mystery of Christ,* so I refer you to that if you want to read more about it.) Suffice it to say here that the image of the mystery appears principally in Ephesians 1 and Colossians 3, and that without it, the heart of Pauline theology stops beating. It's the one word that puts the kibosh on all attempts to read transactional salvation into Paul — and which vindicates his insistence that the redemption of the world is a gift to be trusted, not a deal yet to be closed.

What this image of mystery, of hiddenness, enables these authors to say is that when all is said and done, Paul presents us with two realities which exist simultaneously. The first is the easily perceived and totally undeniable reality of this world as we've corrupted it by our sad mismanagement — by our sins, trespasses, and general failure to do anything that even vaguely resembles God's will for the world he made. That's a creation whose end is death and whose present looks like a tragedy. But the second reality is that same, unreconstructed creation as God has always held it in his beloved Son — in the mystery of the Messiah. That's a world already sprung out of death in his death, already risen in his resurrection, and already seated . . . but we've done that part. The difficulty with this new creation is that it happens to be a world that's unperceivable, utterly deniable, and unsupported by even a shred of observable evidence. It can only be believed, never known. Even the so-called evidences of Jesus' acts prove nothing: his crucifixion doesn't undo the pervasive mayhem of human sin; and after his resurrection, we all go on dying like flies. His victory over sin and death can be "seen" only by faith, not by eyes. But — and this is the genius of Ephesians and Colossians — the world which faith sees is the only one that's going to last because it's the only one God the Word speaks into being forever.

Two realities, then: the first, a leftover piece of human fakery, and the second, the redeemed handiwork of God himself. Two realities, but both co-existing in each other: the mess and the mystery together in the same place; the disaster and the triumph interpenetrating one another — and God himself intimately and immediately present in both, guilty and innocent in both. The evidence for his guilt seems plain enough: omnipotence should be able to do more than just let evil run rampant. And the only evidence for his innocence are his latent fingerprints on the images of Scripture: those conflicted revelations in which he asks us to believe the bizarre assertion that by doing nothing much, he's done it all. In any case, though, the Divine Suspect remains unavailable for cross-examination. He may be responsible for the mess, or the mystery, or both, or neither; but nobody can prove a thing. All we really know is that he says human life is heaven while human life goes on insisting it's hell. The only question for us is, Whose word do we decide to trust? The rest, as Eliot says, is not our business.

≈

I end this chapter with the pitcher who finally clinched the victory in the church's first ball-game, the one who understood Paul as no one else did: the author of the Gospel according to John. The most impressive thing about him is the way in which he brought Paul's theology to completion without seeming to use much if any of Paul's actual work-product — not to mention the way he perfected Mark, Luke, and Matthew without including such pivotal elements as the Birth narratives, the Transfiguration, the institution of the Eucharist, and the Ascension. As I read John's Gospel, his prologue (1:1-18) does duty for the Birth stories; Jesus' dialogue with the Jews at Capernaum (6:22-71) stands in for the institution of the Eucharist; and Jesus' "high-priestly" prayer in chapter 17 (or perhaps even the entire "Last Supper discourse" in chapters 13 through 17) covers the ground of both the Transfiguration and the Ascension.

John, therefore, was a genius, right up there with Paul; and as with all geniuses, his mind wasn't easy to fathom. The New Testament scholar B. S. Easton sums them both up this way: "Paul's real meaning could be grasped only by those who understood his argument as an indivisible whole, a task quite beyond the capacities of almost everyone in the apostolic and sub-apostolic ages . . . [And] the genius of John, like that of Paul, soared far beyond the reach of the rank and file of contemporary Christians."

Most scholars now date the composition of John's Gospel very late indeed: somewhere between 95 and 110, or even later. If that's anywhere near correct, its author was probably in full possession not only of all the Pauline documents but of the Synoptic Gospels as well. In any case, whatever extrapolations, improvements, or corrections he made to those previous works seem to have been added in full confidence that he himself had not only the duty but also the right to have the last word on the subject of Jesus. Witness not only the indirect references to himself in 19:35 and 21:24, but also the sly introduction of "I think" in 21:25 (along with the "it seemed to me" in the preface to Luke, these words are the only two first-person statements by a Gospel author).

All I'm going to do here, however, is give you five instances of the

68

brilliance with which John brought Paul, Colossians, and Ephesians to full fruition.

The first is the solemn prologue that begins his Gospel (1:1-18). Unlike Matthew and Luke, who report Jesus' birth in Bethlehem as the beginning of his career as Lord and Messiah, John goes all the way back to the beginning of everything — in fact, to before the beginning of anything at all, to God before time and space existed:

> ¹In the beginning was the Word, and the Word was with [*pros*, "in the presence of"] God, and the Word was God. ²He was in the beginning with [*pros*] God. [Score one for taking Paul's insight (in 2 Corinthians 4:4) that the Messiah is the image *(eikōn)* of God and running it all the way up the flagpole to the Messiah as God in Person, present to all of creation from the start. Score two for his next tour de force in verses 3 to 5:] ³"All things were made through him, and not a single thing was made without him. What was made ⁴in him [or "by him": *en autō* can mean either] was life, and the life was the light of men [*anthrōpōn*: John is referring to all humanity, not just Israel and not just males]; ⁵and the light shines [*phainei,* present tense] in the darkness, and the darkness did not overcome it.

This is the Word as the actual creator of the world, the One of the Three who, in obedience to the Father's will and over the brooding of the Spirit, speaks creation into being. It's the groundwork for the eventual doctrine of the Trinity; and it's the basis for my frequent insistence that there's nothing anywhere that isn't perpetually held in the arms of the Word and Messiah, who speaks everything into being.

My second instance comes from John 12, where Jesus says, "³¹Now is the judgment [*krisis*] of this world; now the ruler of this world will be cast out; ³²and I, if I be lifted up from the earth, will draw all ["all people," *pantas;* even, in some manuscripts, "all things," *panta*] to myself. ³³This he said, signifying by what kind of death he was about to glorify God." Scores three, four, and five, therefore: three, for John's portrayal of judgment as the *krisis* of grace now rather than the threat of punishment later; four, for emphasizing that the Messiah draws all, not some, to himself; and five, for getting Paul's stress on Jesus' death, all by itself, out from behind the theological trailers (sacrifice, oblation, satisfaction, propitiation, mediation) that threatened to obscure it.

My third instance is what John does with the Pauline phrases *en Christō* and *en autō:* he puts them in the mouth of Jesus himself as *en emoi,* "in me." For example, 6:56: "The one who eats my flesh and drinks my blood remains *in me,* and I in him"; 10:38 and 14:10: "The Father is *in me,* and I am in the Father"; 14:20: "You *in me,* and I in you"; 15:4: "Remain *in me* and I in you; as the branch cannot bear fruit except it remain in the vine, so neither can you, except you remain *in me*"; 16:33: "that *in me* you might have peace"; and last, 17:21: "just as you, Father, are *in me* and I in you, that they also might be one *in us.*" The first six of these verses take the mystery of the Messiah in Paul, Colossians, and Ephesians and put it at the center of Jesus' identity. But the last makes Jesus' relationship with the Father the Envelope, the all-encompassing embrace, in which creation is being carried home to God. Taken together, they open up for us two more images of creation and redemption: Jesus as the Divine Elevator in whom the whole world ascends to the bosom of the Father; and Jesus as the River of love flowing from the Son to the Father: the River (in Psalm 46:4) "whose streams make glad the City of God" — the Divine Mississippi in which we're all inexorably borne into the depths of God himself.

My fourth instance may be the best of all: it's the "I am" passages — all those marvelous repetitions of *ego eimi* that are the crowning achievement of the Gospel of John. Let me simply list the most salient of them for you:

6:35, 48: "I am the bread of life."
6:51: "I am the living bread who comes down from heaven."
8:12: "I am the light of the world."
8:23: "I am from above."
8:24: "Unless you believe that I am [the one], you will die in your sins."
10:7: "I am the door of the sheep."
10:9: "I am the door."

10:11:   "I am the good shepherd."
11:25:   "I am the resurrection and the life."
14:6:   "I am the way, the truth, and the life."
15:1   "I am the true vine."
18:6:   "I am he."

[This last "I am" stands all by itself, with no predicate whatsoever. It's spoken on the night before the crucifixion, and it's said with such force that Judas and the party sent to arrest Jesus are themselves "arrested": they step back and fall flat on the ground.]

My suggestion about these passages is something else that only recently occurred to me — namely, that they can be read as the Johannine equivalents of the parables of Jesus in Matthew, Mark, and Luke. To be sure, John never once uses the word *parable* (*parabolē*, "hard saying," "dark saying") to describe anything Jesus says. On a few occasions, though, he does use an alternative word, *paroimia* (variously translated as "proverb," "figure of speech," "comparison," "hard saying," "parable"). In 10:6, for instance, after Jesus has given his short discourse about the door of the sheepfold (vv. 1-5), John adds, "This *paroimia* Jesus spoke to them; but they didn't know what he was talking to them about." But then John has Jesus do the same trick he so often does in the Synoptic Gospels: when people don't understand one of his hard sayings, he doesn't explain what he meant; he gives them another, even harder saying. In 10:7, Jesus responds to their dumbfoundedness with something more dumbfounding still: "*I am* the door of the sheep."

It was John 10:1-11, in fact, that gave me the idea of interpreting the "I am" passages as Johannine parables. To begin with, they are indeed hard sayings, not simple explanations. Far from turning on the lights in his hearers' minds, they put out any light they may have had. They're not elucidations; they're extinguishings. Next and more important, though, these passages do what the Synoptic parables so regularly do: they move their listeners toward the mystery Jesus is talking about — except that in John, they move them all the way up into the mystery of Jesus himself. In this, they're doing the same job that John's "in me" sayings do: they put Who Jesus Is before anything else. To change the metaphor, the "I am" sayings advance the throttle of

71

the Synoptic parables and fly them to a destination they never quite reached: by recapitulating them in the mouth of Jesus himself, John takes us home to the land of the Trinity.

Last of all, however, is something that I've mentioned often but that becomes supremely clear only in John. Practically every account of something Jesus does or says in the Fourth Gospel ends with someone *believing* in Jesus — that is, trusting, having faith in him. Not in the "signs" he performed or in the "truths" he spoke but purely and simply in him. The changing of water into wine at the wedding in Cana in chapter 2 doesn't conclude with people saying "Wow!" or looking forward to free Chardonnay forever; it ends with the disciples believing in Jesus himself who is "the best wine kept till now." In addition, the cleansing of the Temple in chapter 2 (John moves this event back from Holy Week, where the Synoptics have it, to the beginning of Jesus' ministry) is followed by the assertion that after Jesus' resurrection, the disciples "remembered that he said this, and believed in the Scripture and in the word which Jesus spoke to them" (v. 22). Furthermore, the dialogue with Nicodemus in chapter 3:1-15 ends with the words, "As Moses lifted up the serpent in the wilderness, so must the Son of Man be lifted up, that whoever believes in him may have eternal life." (Just in case you're tempted to argue that people who don't believe are therefore left out in the dark, despite the presence of the Word who is the Light of the World to everyone, see the next chapter, where I'll try to show you how you got that depressing idea.)

John's references, pro or con, to *believing* (the verb's many occurrences in his Gospel derive from the root *pistis,* "faith") continue to appear throughout the Gospel. Jesus' conversation with the Samaritan woman at the well in chapter 4 has an "I am" at verse 26, and it ends with people believing (vv. 39-42). The healing of the crippled man at the pool Beth-zatha in chapter 5 shows us people not believing in him whom the Father has sent (v. 38) and ends with Jesus saying, in verse 46, "If you believed Moses, you would believe me, for he wrote about me. But if you don't believe what he wrote, how will you believe my words?" After the Feeding of the Five Thousand, the people say, "This is the prophet who is coming into the world" (6:14); many believe in him at the Feast of the Tabernacles (7:31); and after

Jesus says, "I am the light of the world" (8:12), many more believe in him (8:30). In chapter 9:35-38, when the man born blind actually sees Jesus for the first time, he says, "I believe," and he worships Jesus. And finally, just before Jesus raises Lazarus from the dead in chapter 11, he says to Lazarus's sister Martha, "I am the resurrection and the life; whoever believes in me, even though he die, yet shall he live; and whoever lives and believes in me will never die." Jesus then asks Martha, "Do you believe this?" And she answers, "Yes, Lord, I believe that you are the Messiah, the Son of God, the one who is coming into the world."

Parenthetically, the raising of Lazarus occurs even before Jesus himself rises from the dead. If any single passage is the death of transactionalism, this is it. Jesus doesn't *do* resurrections, or even *get* himself raised: he *is* the resurrection. Furthermore, even though Jesus said earlier to Martha that "your brother will rise," it's fairly clear that when Jesus finally stands before the tomb and says, "Lazarus, come forth!" he acts as if Lazarus is already alive, even in his grave. (Jesus raised only three people from the dead in the Gospels: the son of the widow at Nain [Luke 7:14], Jairus's daughter [Mark 5:41-42; Luke 8:54], and Lazarus — and all three instances are strikingly mysterious. Jesus does almost nothing to effect these resurrections; he seems simply to have that effect on any dead person he happens to run into. Moreover, no person's "believing" [and certainly no corpse's] is portrayed as the cause of his rising: all the causation lies strictly in the mystery of Jesus himself.)

To finish up, my fifth instance of John's brilliance is a passage that I think has been read wrong almost from the start. It's John 14:6: "*I am* the way, and the truth, and the life; no one comes to the Father but by me." The usual interpretation of the second half of that statement divides the world into two classes of people: those who decide to accept Jesus as their way, truth, and life, and are therefore the beneficiaries of his salvation; and those who don't, and thus are not saved. Even worse, it's been read to say that only practicing Roman Catholics, for example, or proper Missouri Synod Lutherans, or hard-shell Baptists — but certainly not Jews, or Buddhists, or atheists — have Jesus as their ticket to heaven. (To the best of my knowledge, Episcopalians have shied away from that sort of thing;

but maybe that's because a lot of them think only Democrats will be out of luck on the day of judgment.)

The reason such "Christian exclusiveness" is the wrong interpretation of "no one comes to the Father but by me" is simple: the Word who becomes flesh and dwells among us is God himself, the Word by whom all things (not just Republicans) are made. So when Jesus says, "No one comes to the Father but by me," he's talking not about select types who happen to choose him but about the entire human race that's already been chosen by him and in him. And therefore the right way to read this saying of Jesus is to interpret it the same way you would the statement "No mammal can live without air." If that doesn't mean mammals have to decide to breathe air on pain of condemnation (it simply states a fact about all mammalian life), then likewise, no human beings have to select Jesus as their way: they're on the Way no matter what they decide. True, they won't enjoy the trip much if they balk at the ride; but even if they fight it, he's still got them riding with him. Paul got it exactly right: "There is therefore now no condemnation for those who are in Christ Jesus" (Rom. 8:1) — and there's just nobody who isn't in the Word by whom all things are made.

~

Perhaps that will do, though; let me return to the image of the ball game one last time. What John has done, in effect, is turn our full attention to a player I haven't said a thing about until now. I've spent this entire chapter on the pitchers in the church's early games (starters, middle relievers, closers) and on the Divine Manager, the Holy Spirit, who was calling the pitches at every point. But do you realize who actually runs a baseball game on the field? Of course you do: it's the catcher. He's the one who takes the signals from the manager and relays them to whoever happens to be on the mound at the time. A pitcher, of course, may shake off the catcher's signs now and then; but if he doesn't finally give one of them the nod, he'll be out of work in short order. (There's a lesson in this for all the church's subsequent pitchers, preachers and theologians especially included; but I'll leave you to figure that one out for yourself.)

So who, then, is the catcher? In John, it's Jesus himself, out there with his church on the field of play. It was the Divine Catcher who gave the first sign to Saul on the road to Damascus; and it's the Person of the Word Incarnate who's been calling the game in the world ever since Adam. But it's in John that we finally see the Catcher as the Manager's Vicar in the world — or even the Owner's Vicar, if you want to include his references to Jesus and the Father. At last, the "I am" at the center of our being stands forth as the only one from whom we're supposed to take our signals.

PART TWO

A HISTORY
OF SOME IMAGES

FIVE

Mid-season Games and Pitchers

All right; so I lied. That bit about the Catcher wasn't the last reference to baseball — this chapter's title is. With the single comment that by "mid-season" I have in mind the whole nineteen hundred years of theological pitching from John till now, I lay the ball-game imagery down for good.

But since my mind (like the Holy Spirit's, if I may flatter myself) seems to work best when I think in images, here's a less self-congratulatory one for you. What my theological method amounts to is skipping a flat stone across the waters of church history: I don't so much sound the depths of those waters as I bounce off them tangentially. If that strikes you as superficial, be assured you're not alone. More than one reviewer has accused me of being so eager to portray grace as the *crux interpretum* of Scripture that I pass over such important matters as the Bible's ethical injunctions or its call to sanctification of life.

If you're interested, my reason for this supposed lack of balance is that when a five-hundred-pound gorilla is sitting on the other end of your seesaw, you can't get him to play with you by just feeding him bananas. You have to become a six-hundred-pound gorilla and overbalance him. As I see contemporary America from here on Long Island, most people are convinced that the church is in the world to foster religious viewpoints, moral precepts, and family values. But those things are not what the church is here for; they're precisely the five-hundred-pound gorilla that's kept us from getting down to the solid ground of grace, which is the principal piece of real estate we're supposed to be selling. The church is in the world to upset that beast, not encourage it. Grace isn't just a counterpoise to law and order; it's an outrage against them because, like Jesus himself, the church is here not to urge good works on society but to proclaim free forgiveness to the world's riffraff even before they've stopped their nonsense.

Furthermore, overbalancing the beast of works-righteousness was exactly what I was doing when I touched on only selected images in Peter, Paul, Ephesians, Colossians, and John in the previous chapter. I didn't do that because I thought "happier" images might make me popular with the masses; I did it to make clear what I felt was the deepest (and most ignored) thrust of what those apostolic witnesses had to say. But I have company even there: no less an apologist than C. S. Lewis was accused of shallowness. (Academic critics called him a "mere popularizer.") And to be honest, the whole course of my theological writing, such as it's been, has been a matter of skipping stones — of landing lightly on serious subjects. One of my kinder reviewers described my method with an organ-playing metaphor: "Capon executes flights of fancy over a continuing pedal point — over the sustained bass note of grace." Be that as it may, unless you decide to put this book down right now, you're probably stuck with my quirks. On to this chapter's first bounce of the stone.

Irenaeus (c. 130 to 200)

This first of the church's "systematic" theologians was probably born in Asia Minor. In his youth, he had the privilege of meeting and listening to the aged (and eventually martyred) Polycarp (c. 69 to c. 159). But Irenaeus spent almost all of his mature years as a missionary to Gaul and as the bishop of Lugdunum — now Lyons, in southern France. His principal work, *Against the Heresies,* took the form of an exhaustive and sometimes exhausting refutation of the Gnostic speculations that were plaguing the church of his time. (It was originally written in Greek; but except for a few bits that Greek writers quoted from him, it has survived only in an old Latin translation.)

When I noted Polycarp's ninety years in the preceding paragraph, something worth mentioning occurred to me. The much-touted "great distances" between the sub-apostolic writers of the second century and the Apostles themselves shrink dramatically when we're dealing with long lives. Irenaeus had heard Polycarp, who could easily have listened to John or to some other equally authentic early witness — with little lost in the transmission. Let me give you an illustration from my own experience. In my first parish (which I went to in 1949), there was a man named Henry, then in his fifties, who was the first of his father's final four children by a fourth marriage at the age of seventy. If you do the arithmetic on that (1949 minus 50 equals 1899 for Henry's birth date; 1899 minus 70 puts his father's day of birth in the year Andrew Jackson became president), you realize that the stories the old man told the boy Henry about the Civil War period were first-hand eye- or ear-witness accounts. So when I myself (at age twenty-four) heard those stories from Henry, I was only one witness removed from a man who was thirty-four years old when the Battle of Gettysburg was fought. And as you hear this from me in 2000, you're still, nearly 200 years after Henry's father's birth, only two witnesses away from him — and Henry, as far as I know, is still with us!

But back to Irenaeus. The second century was a time of energetic — not to say uncontrolled — theological ferment. Disturbing currents were running below the surface of events. For one thing, the Jewishness of the early *ekklēsia* had all but disappeared, leaving the church a Christian phenomenon more and more in opposition to Judaism. For another, the catholicity of the Jewish *Christos* was vanishing from sight. That insight had been brilliantly expounded by the authors of Colossians and Ephesians as the presence of the mystery of the Messiah in the whole world. (Remember? They said that the Gentiles beyond Judaism had been made Jewish by a circumcision not made with hands.) But soon enough, the bright sun of that universality was totally eclipsed by the satellite notion of the "catholicity of the Christian faith" — conceived of as a body of true doctrine, assented to "everywhere, always, and by all." Adherence to "*the* faith" displaced "trust" in the Incarnate Word's grace as the principal meaning of *pistis*. "Orthodoxy" became the primary meaning of "catholicity."

81

Let me make a parenthesis here to point out a difference between Greek and Latin that bears on this identification of faith with orthodoxy. Greek, like English, possesses a definite article: it can say *hē pistis,* meaning *"the* faith"; or it can use *pistis* all by itself and speak of *faith* pure and simple — that is, *trust* in God's *grace.* (Incidentally, a word with the definite article is said to be in the "arthrous" form, and a word without it is called "anarthrous." Greek is flexible about this, though: *hē pistis* often has to be translated as if it was anarthrous, and *pistis* without the article can sometimes mean *"the* faith.") Latin, however, has no definite article at all: it's an entirely anarthrous language. For example. *Sola fide,* "by faith alone," can mean either "by *trust* alone" or "by *the* faith alone": the translator has to make the decision to omit or supply the definite article. If I'm boring you with this philology lesson, it's only because the confusion of faith with orthodoxy (with *hē didachē,* "the teaching") began as early as the later books of the New Testament. And it eventually turned into a large sleeping dog once Latin became the theological language of the Western church: at the Reformation, it woke up snarling; and ever since, it's been biting Christians right and left. One's faith now commonly means one's beliefs; and "belief" signifies little more than "theological opinion." Here ends the lesson.

In any case, the last three books of Irenaeus's *Against the Heresies* have been called the first systematic exposition of the church's theology. Admittedly, that's slightly misleading. If you read Irenaeus expecting to find a sequentially worked-out "system" of belief, you'll quickly put him down. His contributions to Christian thought don't have the architectural appeal of the propositional wedding cakes produced by later theologians like Thomas Aquinas and the successors of Luther and Calvin. You come upon them as delightful surprises, and you savor them as raisins, currants, and candied peel in an otherwise dull pudding of Gnostic blather. Tiresome as the pudding may be, though, Irenaeus remains one of our principal sources for what the Gnostics actually taught. (The church generally saw to it that their writings were destroyed, which is a shame, because some of their insights had already been put to good theological use in Colossians, Ephesians, and even in Irenaeus himself — and others still might be if only we had access to them.)

82

Chief among Irenaeus's contributions, at least for me, is his ringing emphasis on the Incarnation of the Word as the heart of Christian thought. It's even fair to say that he proclaimed the centrality of the Incarnation more than two centuries before the church got around to defining the doctrines of the Trinity and the Incarnation in the Conciliar Period. And then, of course, there's his stress on recapitulation. That image, as I've already noted, was rooted in the truth that the Word (the *Logos*) who becomes flesh to redeem the world is also the God by whom all things are made. For Irenaeus, both creation and redemption occur in the Word himself. Adam is the first creature redeemed in Jesus' death, and the entire history of the world is recapitulated in Jesus' resurrection. Irenaeus doesn't depict the Word as a late arrival trying to catch up with the accidents of history; all of history is in his Person from the beginning. (To ring yet another change on Harnack, no one in the second century understood John better than Irenaeus.) Furthermore, his mind was completely at home with images of his own devising. One of the most brilliant of those was his presentation of the Son and the Holy Spirit as the "two hands of God," which was an image of the Trinity before the church ever got around to defining the Three in One. Here, then, are a few samples of his work; I think you'll find them at least as illuminating as anything in the Nicene Creed.

First, one of my favorite fingerprints of the Divine Suspect — the image of *recapitulation*. In *Against the Heresies,* Book V, chapter 14, Irenaeus has been speaking of all the blood that has been shed, from the murder of Abel to Jesus' own times, and he finally comes to the words of Jesus himself: "Verily I say to you, all these things shall come upon this generation." He then continues:

[Jesus] thus points out the recapitulation of the effusion of blood from the beginning that would take place in his own Person, [the recapitulation of the blood] of all the righteous men and of the prophets; and [he also points out] that by means of himself there would be a requisition of their blood. . . . For the Lord [Jesus as the Word of God], taking dust from the earth, molded man; and it was on [mankind's] behalf that all the dispensation of the Lord's advent took place. He himself, therefore, possessed flesh and blood, recapitulating in himself not some other being, but that original handiwork of the Father, seeking out the thing that had perished.

Next, consider the following passage on the *two Hands* of God the Father (the Son and the Holy Spirit) in Book V, chapter 1:

As at the beginning of our formation in Adam, that breath of life which proceeded from God, having been united to what had been fashioned, animated the man and manifested him as a being endowed with reason; so also in [the times of] the end, the Word of the Father and the Spirit of God, having become united with the ancient substance of Adam's formation, rendered man living and perfect, receptive of the perfect Father, in order that as in the natural [Adam] we were all dead, so in the spiritual we may all be made alive. For never at any time did Adam [humankind] escape the Hands of God [Word and Spirit] — to [which Hands] the Father [was] speaking when he said 'Let *Us* make man [*the adam*] in *Our* image, after *Our* likeness. And for this reason, in the last times, not by the will of the flesh nor by the will of man, but by the good pleasure of the Father, his Hands formed a living man in order that Adam might be created [again] after the image and likeness of God.

Just one more passage, for the pure fun of Irenaeus's imagery, when he deals with Jesus' healing of *the man born blind* in Book V, chapter 15:

To that man . . . he gave sight . . . that he might show forth the Hand of God which at the beginning had molded man. . . . And therefore when his disciples asked him why the man had been born blind [Jesus] replied, "Neither has this man sinned nor his parents; [this happened so] that the works of God might be made manifest in him." For the work of God is the fashioning of man. For as the Scripture says [Genesis 2:7], he made man by a kind of process: "And the Lord took clay from the earth and formed man." Wherefore also the Lord [Jesus] spat on the

ground and made clay and smeared it on the eyes, pointing out
how the original fashioning [of man] was effected, and manifest-
ing the Hand of God to those who can understand by what
Hand man was formed from the dust. For that which the Artifi-
cer, the Word, had omitted to form in the womb [namely, the
blind man's eyes], he then supplied in public, that the works of
God might be manifested in him, in order that we might not be
seeking out another hand by which man was fashioned, nor another Father — [and that we might know] that this Hand of God
[that is, the Word] which formed us at the beginning, and which
does form us in the womb, has in the last times sought out us
who were lost, winning back his own and taking up the lost
sheep on his shoulders, and with joy restoring it to the fold of
life.

But we owe Irenaeus still more: he's the first major Christian
thinker to set forth almost the entire canon of the New Testament.
In fact, he's the first to raise the writings of the New Testament to
the level of *Scripture*. As you know, no contemporaries of Paul, Mark,
Luke, Matthew, or John recognized their work as Scripture when it
first came out, or even after it had been around for a while. Up until
the time of Irenaeus, the word *Scripture* denoted the Hebrew Bible
only, usually in the LXX version. Even in Irenaeus's day, there were
no copies of the New Testament as such lying around. The books we
now revere existed separately in various manuscripts, of course; but
they existed chiefly *in the minds* of those who cherished them.

To read Irenaeus is to be stunned by his prodigious memory. It was
something he shared with almost every educated person of his day —
and of every other day until now, when memorization has ceased to be
one of the main tools of learning. The older boys and girls of the
church knew vast tracts of Scripture by heart. They didn't have
printed Bibles in which they could look verses up. They didn't have
concordances to remind them of passages they'd forgotten. The
Scriptures were in their heads, and the concordances were in the syn-
apses of their brains. Even when Irenaeus makes a mistake (for example, when he refers to the child of Jairus whom Jesus raised as the
"daughter of the high priest"), it's not that he failed to consult the

text; it's just that he heard the text in his mind's ear and momentarily switched *archiereus,* "high priest," for *archisynagōgos,* "ruler of the synagogue." Even in his errors, therefore, his memory puts ours to shame. We hardly have enough wit to remember eggs, cheddar, broccoli, and chicken in the supermarket without a written list.

Moreover, it's Irenaeus who quotes from all the books of the New Testament except Hebrews, 3 John, and Jude — and as I said, he quotes them as if they were on a par with the books of the Hebrew canon. Not only that, but he's the first orthodox writer who treats the present "four" as the only authentic Gospels. Alas, though, he doesn't do as well by the Apostles' Creed. By his time, that "baptismal symbol" had been around, in one form or another, for a good while. But in his hands its significance underwent a subtle change. Originally, it had been a shorthand formulation of the mysteries of the Messiah to whom the faith of believers was addressed. But in Irenaeus, it starts to lose its character as a recitation of mysteries and begins to be a standard of doctrine for the refutation of heresy. Like all great innovators, he himself wasn't thrown off his stride by this: he continued to revel in the mystery of it all. But the trend he started took root and grew wildly. The Councils watered it; the medieval church turned it into the aggressive crabgrass of scholastic theology; the Reformers' confessions of faith encouraged it to run rampant over the church's front yard; and we're still trying to get it out of our theological lawns. But perhaps that will do for Irenaeus. Time for the next skip of the stone.

Athanasius (c. 296 to 373)

Athanasius is best known for his almost forty years of resistance to the Arian heresy at and after the Council of Nicaea in 325. The Arians held that the Son of God, the Word of the Father, was not God himself but only a creature whom God had made out of nothing before he made anything else. The Word, they held, could not be God because God is unique and his essence cannot be shared with any merely created being. Jesus, while certainly worthy of worship, could be called God in name only and not in substance. Therefore, when they tried to deal with the Fourth Gospel's statement that "the

Word was God" (John 1:1), they read it in a purely honorific sense, not as a statement of the Word's equality with the Father. The Arians took their name from Arius, a presbyter of Alexandria, whose catch phrase for this interpretation was "*There was* [an occasion, a situation, a "once"] *when he* [the Word] *was not*" [*ēn hote ouk ēn*]. He was careful not to say "There was a *time* when he was not," since he considered the Word to have been begotten by the Father before all time; but he refused to say that the Word was "of one being with the Father." And it was this refusal that Athanasius, resting his case squarely on John, opposed for most of his life. That opposition (and the many periods of exile he suffered because of it) won him the label *Athanasius contra mundum* "Athanasius against the world."

He was born in Egypt, most probably in 296, of wealthy Christian parents; but his education made him a thoroughgoing Greek. Small of stature but with a towering understanding of the faith in which he had been raised, he blossomed very early indeed. He was about seven years old when the last persecution began (under the Emperor Diocletian) in 303; he was seventeen when the church was made a *religio licita*, a tolerated religion, by the edict of Constantine in 313; and he was about twenty-four when he wrote his two principal works, *Contra Gentes*, "Against the Gentiles," and *De Incarnatione Verbi Dei*, "On the Incarnation of the Word of God." He attended the renowned Catechetical School at Alexandria in his early teens; and well before he wrote those two books, he became a member of the household of Alexander, the Patriarch of Alexandria. He attended the Council of Nicaea in 325 as a non-voting deacon and adviser to Alexander, and he was elected to succeed him as Bishop of Alexandria in 328 (having just barely reached the canonical age of thirty). He served in that post (often *in absentia*) for the rest of his life, dying in 373.

Athanasius's writings are neither speculative nor particularly original. That in fact is their beauty. They present us with a brilliant mind totally committed to the classic truths of the church — to the *tradition* he had received from the already longish line of Apostles, Martyrs, and Bishops who came before him. He's a witness not to his own insights but to what he saw as the teaching of the church from the beginning. He writes as an expositor, not a controversialist: like the "scribe instructed in the kingdom of heaven" in Matthew 13:52, he is precisely the church's "master of the house," bringing forth out of his treasure "things new and old." We read him not so much to learn what was going wrong in the church of his time as to learn how the church catholic had picked up on the fingerprints of God from the start.

My principal concern here will be with his *De Incarnatione*. In the original Greek, the title is *Peri tēs Enanthrōpoiseōs tou Logou,* "Concerning the Word's *Becoming Human*" — *enanthrōpoiseōs* ("en-man-ment") being rather a better word than the Latin *incarnatio* ("en-fleshment"). As I read him, he stands with John and Irenaeus in the great tradition of those who put Who Jesus Is as the Person of the Word of God before the secondary considerations of what Jesus did to save the world, or what he said to instruct it. I'm going to give you a sample of his approach; but first, a short preface to set the stage for the quotations.

In *De Incarnatione,* Athanasius has been dealing with the dilemma that confronted God as a result of human sin. On the one hand, God had said to Adam, "Of every tree of the garden you may freely eat; but of the tree of the knowledge of good and evil you shall not eat, for in the day that you eat of it you shall surely die." But on the other hand, what followed that threat (that sentence of death from God) was *corruption:* the wasting away, the disappearance, for all practical purposes, of the reasonable and good human race that God had created in the beginning. What was God to do, Athanasius asks, about such a disastrous reversal of his plans? Could he be content just to accept repentance as the cure for human sin? Or was something more necessary? Here is how Athanasius answers those questions (*De Incarnatione* VII, 4-5):

> If it was only that a mistake had been made [on the part of human beings] and not a matter of the *corruption* that followed it, then repentance might well have solved the problem. But the real problem was that once the human race had been overtaken by its transgression, people were by their very nature held in bondage to the ensuing corruption and had lost the grace they had by being made in the image of God. So what else had to be

done? Or better said, *of whom* was there a need if such a work of grace and re-calling was to be done, if not of the *Word of God* who even from the beginning had made the whole world out of nothing? He alone was the one who could both bring the corruptible to incorruption and restore to the Father his reputation of self-consistent fairness toward all. And that was because, being the Word of the Father, and being over all, he was naturally the only one who was able to recreate the whole world, to suffer on behalf of all, and to be the ambassador who could present to the Father a sufficient reparation for all.

Note how close Athanasius stands to John and Irenaeus in all this. For him, it's the Word's relationship with the Father that makes the world go round, both in creation and redemption. Unlike Anselm or the medieval and Reformation theologians who followed him, he puts the Horse of the Incarnation of the Word before the cart of Atonement. He doesn't envision the Son as an intermediary making a sufficient satisfaction to an offended Father. Rather, he roots both the creation and the redemption of the world in the *philanthrōpia* of the Word as God himself — that is, in his sheer love for humankind as it was perpetually declared in the bosom of the Father from the beginning. For Athanasius, if I may repeat myself, the reconciliation of the human race springs not out of something the Word did at one point in time but out of Who He Is before, during, and after all time. He is the Father's Word by whom all things are made, not a divine tradesman sent to repair the damage done by sin. He comes not to replace a broken world with a better one but to restore the world he loves to what he had in mind for it all along.

In this respect, Athanasius turns out to be in company not only with the church catholic before his time but with the common wisdom of the pre-medieval theologians who followed him. To be honest, I came to read him only recently — long after I had imbibed his spirit from the ancient hymnody of the church. One hymn in particular has stuck in my mind for almost fifty years: a Latin acrostic poem on the life of Christ written by Sedulius (around 450). Here are the two opening stanzas, both in the original and in a fairly literal prose translation:

A solis ortus cardine	From lands that see the sun arise
ad usque terrae limitem	to earth's remotest boundary,
Christum canamus Principem	we sing our praise of Christ the King,
natum Maria Virgine.	born of Mary, Virgin pure.
Beatus Auctor saeculi	Though blessed Author of the world,
servile corpus induit,	he put a servant's body on;
ut carne carnem liberans	that liberating flesh by flesh,
non perderet quos condidit.	he might not lose those whom he made.

I think it was this hymn, lurking in the back of my mind, that eventually led me to appreciate the image of recapitulation in Ephesians and Irenaeus. And that in turn was what led me to the image of the Word's retelling of all our history — of his speaking the human race into being at the beginning, of our contradiction of that speaking in sin, and of his counter-speaking of our contradiction. In any case, as I now see those "three acts," they're not sequential events but one simultaneous and perpetual act of creation and redemption — one age-long declaration of our true being to the Father. As Athanasius so charmingly puts it (VIII, 1),

> This indeed was why the bodiless, incorruptible, and immaterial Word of God came into our territory. He certainly didn't come because he was previously far away, since not a single part of the creation had ever been left empty of him who, while ever abiding in union with the Father, yet fills all things that are. But now he is present to us, stooping to our level by his love [*philanthrōpia*] and self-revealing [*epiphania*] toward us.

And that, if you think about it, is exactly what Sedulius had in mind when he said that the Word came so he might not lose what he made. The Word of God is not a plumber sent by the home office to snake out drains in the suburbs of creation. He's the blessed Author of all things who's "got the whole world in his hands." He comes to customers he never left; and he comes only to do what he never stopped doing. His coming, therefore, is not a transaction of any kind; it's just another chapter in "the same old story/of Jesus and his love."

Just a few more samples of Athanasius's clarity and we can move on. First, an example of the way he puts the *identity* of the Incarnate Word in front of all the parked trailers that later writers were stuck in when they preoccupied themselves with explanations of how the Word managed to do the work of redemption. He does indeed use the language of offering, sacrifice, and substitution; but, unlike his successors, he never loses sight of the truth that it's the Person of the Word, not his incidental deeds or sayings, who liberates us from death (IX, 1-2):

> For the Word saw at a glance that the corruption of the human race could not be gotten rid of otherwise than through death, even though the Word himself, being immortal and the Son of the Father, could not die. Because of this, he took to himself a body capable of death so that such a body, by its participation in the Word who is above all, might be a stand-in for all — and so that, on account of the indwelling of the Word, it might remain incorruptible and as a result put an end to corruption for all others by the grace of the resurrection. Accordingly, he took this body to himself as an offering and sacrifice free from every stain; and he brought it to death, thus making death disappear [*ēphanize* — he "disappeared" it] from all his human brethren by the offering of himself in their stead. For naturally [*eikotōs*, "authentically," "appropriately" — from *eikōn*: "icon," "image," even "sacrament" of God himself], since the Word of God was above all, and since he offered his own temple and bodily instrument on behalf of all, he offered that body as a living sacrament [*antipsychon*] for all and fulfilled in death all that was required. And since he was one in being with all human nature, the incorruptible Son of God appropriately [*eikotōs* again] clothed all with incorruption by the promise of the resurrection. For the solidarity of the human race is such that, by virtue of the Word's indwelling in a single human body, the corruption that goes with death has lost its power over all.

My penultimate quote from Athanasius is offered to show you how deeply rooted in Scripture his mind was. As a matter of fact, the earliest extant list we have of the books of the New Testament as they now stand appears in his 39th Festal (Easter) Letter, written in 367. He's thus the first father of the church who can be proved to have been working with a full deck. As you'll see, he played his cards like an expert (X, 1-5, selections):

This great work was indeed supremely worthy of the goodness of God. A king who has founded a house or city, far from neglecting it when through the carelessness of the inhabitants it is attacked by robbers, avenges it and saves it from destruction, having more regard to his own honor than to the people's neglect. Much more then, the God who was the Word of the all-good Father was not unmindful of the human race he had made to exist; rather, by the offering of his own body, he abolished the death that they had incurred and corrected their neglect by his own teaching. Thus by his own power he restored all things human. And that these truths were believed even by the Savior's own inspired disciples can be proved by anyone who is conversant with their writings: [For example, 2 Cor. 5:14-15]: "For the love of Christ urges us on, because we are convinced that one died for all; and that therefore all have died. And he died for all so that we who live might live no longer for ourselves but for him who died and rose from the dead for us, our Lord Jesus Christ." And again [Heb. 2:9]: "But we see Jesus, who for a little while was made lower than the angels, now crowned with glory and honor because of the suffering of death, so that by the grace of God, he might taste death for all."

The same writer also points out why it was necessary for God the Word himself to become Incarnate [*enanthrōpoisai*]: "For it was fitting for him, on whose account all things exist and through whom all things are made, in bringing many sons to glory, to make the pioneer of their salvation perfect through sufferings" [Heb. 2:10]. This he says, signifying that the restoration of the human race from corruption could be accomplished by none other than the Word of God who had made it in the first place. And the Word took a body to himself so that it might be a sacrifice for other bodies like his. . . . And he signifies this by saying: "Since then the children had become sharers of flesh and blood, he himself also participated in the same, in order that through death he might destroy the one who has the power of death, that is, the devil, and set free those who all their lives were held in slavery by the fear of death" [Heb. 2:14-15]. . . .

For by the sacrifice of his own body, he did two things: he put an end to the law of death that stood against us; and he made a new beginning of life for us by giving us the hope of the resurrection. For since it was by human beings [*ex anthrōpōn*] that death came to have power over humanity [*eis anthrōpous*], it was therefore by the human Incarnation [*enanthrōpoiseōs*] of the Word of God that there came about the destruction of death and the resurrection of life — which is exactly what Paul, the Christ-bearer, says: "For since death comes in through a human being [*di' anthrōpou*], the resurrection of the dead also comes in through a human being [*di' anthrōpou*]; for as in Adam all die, so also in Christ all shall be made alive, and so forth" [1 Cor. 15:21-22].

So we no longer die now as condemned; rather, as raised from the dead we await the common resurrection of all, "which in his own times he will show" [1 Tim. 6:15], namely, God the Word who wrought this resurrection and freely bestowed on us its benefits.

As with Irenaeus, my final citation from Athanasius is meant to give you a taste of his way with imagery. In chapter XXV, 3-5 of *De Incarnatione*, he's speaking of the curse of the law under which Christ died, and he's just quoted Deuteronomy 21:23: "Cursed is every one who hangs on a tree." Here's what he does with that:

3. . . . Therefore, if the death of the Lord is a ransom for all, and by his death the "middle wall of partition" is broken down, and if the calling of the Gentiles is a fact, how else then would he call us to himself unless he was crucified? For it is only on a cross that a person dies with outstretched hands. Therefore it was fitting for the Lord to undergo even this, and to stretch out his hands, so that with the one hand he might draw his ancient people [Israel], and with the other draw the Gentiles, joining both together in himself.

And then, picking up on the description of the devil as the ruler of the power of the air *(aëros)*, which now works in the children of disobedience, he runs with that image:

> 5. . . . The Lord came that he might cast down the devil and cleanse the air, and make a way up to heaven for us, as the Apostle says, "through the veil," that is, through his flesh. This had to happen by death. But by what other death could this have come about than by a death that happened in the air? For nobody dies in the air except someone who expires on a cross. Therefore the Lord also underwent this with the utmost appropriateness.

All in all, nobody handles Scripture better than Athanasius. But there were others in the fourth and fifth centuries who labored to do it similar justice — and that brings us to the last skip of the stone in this chapter.

The Four Great Councils (325 to 451)

The history of what is now called the Conciliar Period is the story of a contest over words: a battle for the possession of certain paradoxical images and for the elimination of others that ranged from merely plausible to downright wrong. I'm well aware that it's usually viewed as a fight over concepts — even as an attempt to make propositional statements about the church's teaching long before that way of doing theology had become the *idée fixe* of Christian thinking. But I think that's wrong. True enough, the words that were brandished in the war (such as *ousia,* meaning "substance," "essence," or "being," and *hypostasis,* meaning "substance" "essence," or "person") were common in the Greek thought of the time. But since the church was arguing about how these words might apply to the three Persons of the Trinity or to the Incarnation of God the Word in the *Christos* — and since all of those "objects of discourse" were about mysteries that were not directly perceivable by human minds — it seems to me that the words with which the church was trying to describe those mysteries are better understood if we think of them as images, as "word pictures," rather than as tightly defined philosophical terms.

94

For it was precisely their definitions that were the problem: there was wide disagreement among theologians of the time as to how those words were to be understood. To be sure, some of the participants in the Councils rejected the heretical images out of hand, simply because they were unscriptural — mere borrowings from secular thought. But even among those willing to allow their use, there were divergent interpretations of their meaning. For the very reason that they were being used as images of mysteries, the struggle wasn't really over what the terms themselves meant; it was about which was the best image for a given mystery — about which shed the most light in the darkness of conflicting opinion.

In other words, the orthodox party was trying to produce a vocabulary of images that would hold still long enough to give sharp pictures of the Father, Son, and Holy Spirit as one God and of the *Christos* as the Word of God Incarnate. Accordingly, it was all new work. Like the re-imaging of the sacrificial system of the Old Testament in Hebrews — or like Thomas Aquinas's christianization of Aristotle's vocabulary — it was the creation of a new way of seeing the old truths the church had held for centuries. It was (if you'll allow me an anachronism) a very "modern" thing to do: at the Councils, the fathers of the church took over a secular vocabulary and baptized it. In fact, they did exactly what advocates of modernity are now urging us to do: they made the church "relevant" to their own age.

The first four such gatherings of the church (now called the General or the Ecumenical Councils) took place at Nicaea in 325, at Constantinople in 381, at Ephesus in 431, and at Chalcedon in 451. One note on the word *ecumenical*. In our own day the word has slipped away from its original meaning: it now means little more than "interchurch" or even "interreligious." But at the time of the Councils it was used to denote the "worldwideness" of the church catholic. *Ecumenical* comes from the Greek *oikoumenē*, a word used to describe what the fathers thought of as the civilized world of the time — namely, the *orbis terrarum*, the "circle of lands" around the Mediterranean where the church, East and West, held sway. Note too that for a Council to be called "ecumenical," it did not have to have representation from both East and West. (The gathering in Constantinople, in fact, was attended only by Eastern bishops.) Ecumenicity, therefore, was not a quality built into the fiber of Councils as institutions. And it certainly wasn't like the papal infallibility that Pius IX defined in 1870: a quality that "kicked in" automatically once certain requirements for institutional proclamation had been met. Nor was any particular Council ever recognized as ecumenical the minute it wrapped up its work. Ecumenicity was strictly an *ex post facto* matter. It was only by looking back over time that the church pronounced any given Council "ecumenical."

Specifically, what these Councils were trying to do was produce creeds, or creedal statements, that would represent the authentic belief of the church from the beginning. (*Creed* is from *credo,* "I believe.") By the exigencies of the times, these statements most often came out as refutations of heresy. In this, of course, they stood at a considerable distance from the original purpose of the Apostles' Creed. Still, the very strength and popularity of the heresies provided the Councils with an excuse of sorts: the church, they felt, was being challenged to say clearly what it did and didn't believe. The impression of theological nit-picking that the Councils now leave in the minds of some isn't really the fault of the Councils: the nits were everywhere, and they were not only annoying but dangerous.

Now for some examples of the work-product of the Councils, beginning with Nicaea 325. When that Council began (under the presidency of the Emperor Constantine himself), Eusebius, the Bishop of Caesarea (and something of a wily politician), took the initiative and tried to get the Council to adopt the creed of his own church as its considered judgment. Here is how that creed read:

> We believe in one God, the Father All-sovereign, the maker of all things visible and invisible;
>
> And in one Lord Jesus Christ, the Word of God, God of God, light of light, Son only-begotten, Firstborn of all creation, begotten of the Father before all the ages, through whom also all things were made; who was made flesh for our salvation and lived among men, and suffered, and rose again on the third day, and ascended to the Father, and shall come again in glory to judge the living and the dead;
>
> We believe also in one Holy Spirit.

Eusebius was orthodox enough, but his creed didn't explicitly address the Arian opinions that were rapidly spreading through the church at the time — and which continued to flourish for a number of centuries thereafter. Thus, when the Council of Nicaea met, it labored to produce a version of Eusebius's creed that would correct the Arian errors. (Another note, this time on the spellings of "Nicaea" and "Nicene":"Nicaea" is the name of a city, and "Nicene" is the designation of a creed. As you'll see, the "Creed of Nicaea" is not what we presently call the "Nicene Creed." Our current version is actually the work of Constantinople 381 and should properly be called the "Nicaeno-Constantinopolitan Creed.") In any case, here is what the fathers at Nicaea actually came up with. (The words in brackets are their additions and alterations.)

> We believe in one God, the Father All-sovereign, maker of all things visible and invisible;
> And in one Lord Jesus Christ, the Son of God, *begotten of the Father,* only begotten, *that is, of the substance of the Father* [*ek tēs ousias tou patros*], God of God, Light of Light, *true God of true God, begotten not made, of one substance with the Father* [*homoousion tō patri*], through whom all things were made, *things in heaven and things on earth;* who for us men and for our salvation *came down* and was made flesh, *and became man* [*enanthrōpēsanta*], suffered, and rose on the third day, ascended into the heavens, and is coming to judge living and dead;
> And in the Holy Spirit.

Just a word about the phrases in brackets. *Ek tēs ousias tou patros* means "out of the *ousia,* the inmost being of the Father" — that is, inseparably one with the Father's essence. *Homoousion tō patri* means "of the *same* being with the Father," that is, sharing one and the same *ousia* ("substance," "essence") with the Father — in other words, essentially one with him while existentially distinct from him. (Arius was willing to say only that the Son was *homoiousion tō patri,* of *similar* being with the Father.) Finally, *enanthrōpēsanta,* Athanasius's word for "Incarnation," means "taking on himself all that makes man human." In effect, it clarified Eusebius's word *sarkothenta,* "was made flesh" — which had left the door open for some to deny that the Word had taken human nature into his Person, and to view the humanity of Jesus as a transitory disguise that the Word put on. The Council may even have felt that Eusebius's phrase "lived among men" (*en anthrōpois politeusamenon,* "conversing among men," "associating with men") had the same defect.

In any case, approval of the Creed of Nicaea was included in the proclamation of the Council of Chalcedon by its reference to "the faith of the three-hundred-fifteen fathers" who were at Nicaea 325, right along with a similar endorsement of "the faith of the one-hundred-fifty fathers" (the Nicaeno-Constantinopolitan Creed, 381). But at the time of its adoption, the Creed of Nicaea settled very little. Not only was it the work of a minority at Nicaea itself; but Arianism continued to spread throughout the church, attracting those who were still worrying the bone of the relationship between the Son and the Father in the Trinity. More importantly, though, the largely unaddressed question of the relationship between the Divine and human natures in Christ himself began to take center stage as the next major point of controversy. Paul, Colossians, and Ephesians may have dealt brilliantly with the question of Who Christ Is, and John may have put the finishing touches on their work. But in theology, the last word seldom gets said. The mystery of Christ is a slippery piece of business: for everyone who can grasp it with a suitable image, there will always be dozens whose images can't get a grip on it. Which, naturally enough, brings us to the three remaining ecumenical Councils.

Constantinople 381 dealt primarily with a heresy that went by the name of Apollinarianism — after Apollinarius, a Bishop of Laodicea who died around 392, and who may or may not have been an Apollinarian himself. In any event, none of his works has come down to us. All we have are bits and pieces quoted by his adversaries; his actual writings were suppressed, as such books generally were in those times, by the eventually triumphant orthodox party. That, unfortunately, was the "dark side" of the Conciliar Period — and of much of the rest of ecclesiastical history: book-burning (not to mention heretic-burning) continued to be an outdoor sport in the church up to and including the Reformation era.

But despite the church's fondness for playing the controlling mother who confiscates her children's naughty reading matter, it's never been a good or even a workable idea. You may put heretical books out of print; but you can't stop clever minds from re-inventing the heresies from scratch. The very plausibility of most heresies makes them easier to grasp, and to sell, than orthodoxy. For the essence of heresy isn't a fondness for wrong ideas. It's a preference ("heresy" is from *hairein,* "to take," "to select") for one aspect of a truth over the paradoxical wholeness of that truth. As someone once said, "The opposite of a great truth isn't a falsehood; it's another great truth." Heresy mistakes the apparent conflict of paradoxical images for contradiction; orthodoxy revels in the complementarity, even in the coincidentality of those images. Good theology never shies away from the *coincidentia oppositorum.*

Apollinarianism was just such a shying away. Unlike Arianism, it accepted the Deity of God the Son and all the language that the Creed of Nicaea applied to him. It was perfectly willing to say that he was the only begotten Son of the Father, God of God, Light of Light, true God of true God, begotten not made, of one substance *(homoousion)* with the Father, et cetera. But when Apollinarianism tried to deal with the paradoxical image of the union of the Divine and human in Christ, it allowed a contradiction to dominate its thinking.

By the time of the Council of Constantinople, the focus of ecclesiastical debate had shifted. It was no longer about the Trinity itself but about whether Christ was both truly God and completely human — and in particular, about whether the Word who became completely human in Jesus was the very Person of his humanity or just some kind of additive that substantially altered it. And it was on that last point that Apollinarianism made its misstep. It was an ingenious, even a plausible error; but it was a fatal one nonetheless. The Apollinarians held that God had indeed arranged for the *Logos,* the Word of the Father, to become one with Jesus; but they said that God achieved that oneness by replacing the human soul of Jesus (his rational soul, or mind) with God the Word himself.

In short, the Apollinarians let their enthusiasm for the Deity of Christ lead them to denigrate his humanity. They explained the union of God and man in Christ by fiddling with his manhood to the point of making it unrecognizable as human anymore. When they got done with Jesus, he didn't have a complete, or perfect *(telea)*, or unalloyed human nature; instead, his humanity became a theological scrambled egg in which the Divine Yolk was utterly blended into the human white. Or, to put it another way, they turned Christ into Clark Kent — a person who wasn't much of a human being to begin with and who couldn't really become Superman until he went into the phone booth and became a jazzed-up version of humanity. (Remember? In the original stories, Superman had powers beyond those of mortal men, but he could use them only at the price of a sexless relationship with Lois Lane. In the later TV series, this was improved slightly by having Clark/Superman court and marry Lois, and by turning Lois into something smarter than the most clueless woman on the planet; but our hero still needed to get rid of his human clothes before he could be the interplanetary savior.)

As far back as the second century, Tertullian had put all such humanity-altering nonsense out of its misery by pointing out that it made Christ the Savior into a *tertium quid,* a "third something-or-other" which, while it might still truly be God, was certainly not like any human being you could run into at a PTA meeting. And at Constantinople in 381 the orthodox party said much the same thing. Witness Gregory of Nazianzus, Archbishop of Constantinople: "If anyone has put his trust [in Christ] as a man without a human mind, he is himself devoid of mind. . . . For what [the Word] has not assumed he has not healed." Or, as another formulation had it, "If he wasn't God, he couldn't *save* us; and if he wasn't completely human, he couldn't save *us.*"

Constantinople, however, was not the end of the controversy over the Person of Christ. The Council of Ephesus in 431 had to deal with yet another heresy — namely, the refusal of the Nestorians (after Nestorius, another "disappeared" writer) to accept the title of *theotokos* for the Virgin Mary. *Theotokos* means "God bearer." (In Latin, it came out as *mater Dei,* "mother of God.") To many people's ears, this pet phrase of the orthodox sounds extravagant, even blasphemous. But what it meant to those who espoused it wasn't that Mary was the mother of God as God, but that the Person born of the

Virgin was truly and undeniably God the Word himself. Properly grasped, it said nothing more than what we still say at Christmas when we sing of the Infant Jesus in the hymn *Adeste fideles:* "God of God, Light from Light eternal, / lo! he abhors not the Virgin's womb." The fact that we also believe him to be genuinely human can never be used as a pretext for welshing on his Divinity.

Thus the Council of Ephesus, bizarre as its insistence on *theotokos* might seem if you take it as an exercise in propositional theology, becomes a perfect example of my contention that the Councils were doing theology by way of images. "Mother of God" isn't a definition that gives us answers to our questions; it's a sudden illumination of the fact that in Mary, the images of Son, Word, God, Man, and Womb all come together in a new coincidence of opposites. And if you take that paradoxical picture as a seamless whole, you absolve yourself from having to water down any of those images. Precisely because you're not trying to wring some plausible answer out of their apparent contradiction, they free you to arrive at a clearer view of the real question about the Word made flesh. And that question — as I've said many times already and will continue to say again and again — is simply this: *Who* is this Jesus in whom we believe?

It was the Council of Chalcedon in 451 that gave us the definitive set of images for grasping Who He Is. The heresy it addressed went by the name of Monophysitism (from *monos*, "one," and *physis*, "nature"). Eutyches, a leader of the Monophysites, had held that in Christ there was a single, *theandric* nature (*the-* for God and *andr-* for man) — a "God-mannish" nature in which his manhood had effectively been turned into a souped-up version of humanity (shades of the scrambled egg, the Clark Kent of the Apollinarians, and Tertullian's *tertium quid*). I shall quote the "Definition of Chalcedon" for you in a moment. But let me urge you once again to try and see its use of philosophically tinged Greek notions more as a matter of playing with images than as reasoning by means of concepts. That might be a bit of a stretch, I admit. But if "water," "light," "tree," "blood," and "rock" can be made into images of the Incarnate Word, why can't "nature," "confusion," "change," "division," and "separation" be put to use as well? At any rate, here is the text of the Chalcedonian Definition. (Please note, if you haven't already: the fathers of the church, not having been brought up on modern style manuals, didn't share our fear of run-on sentences.)

> Therefore, following the holy Fathers, we all with one accord teach men to acknowledge one and the same Son, our Lord Jesus Christ, at once complete in Godhead and complete in manhood, truly God and truly man, consisting also of a reasonable [*logikēn*] soul and body; of one substance [*homoousios*] with the Father as regards his Godhead, and at the same time of one substance with us as regards his manhood; like us in all respects, apart from sin; as regards his Godhead, begotten of the Father before the ages, but yet as regards his manhood begotten, for us men and for our salvation, of Mary the Virgin, the God-bearer [*theotokos*]; one and the same Christ, Son, Lord, Only-begotten, recognized in two natures [*en duo physesin*], without confusion [*asygchytōs*], without change [*atreptōs*], without division [*adiairetōs*], without separation [*achōristōs*]; the distinction of natures being in no way annulled by the union, but rather the characteristics of each nature being preserved and coming together to form one person and subsistence [*hypostasis*], not as parted or separated into two persons, but one and the same Son and Only-begotten God the Word, Lord Jesus Christ; even as the prophets from earliest times spoke of him, and our Lord Jesus Christ himself taught us, and the creed of the Fathers has handed down to us.

This is a brilliant, resourceful juggling of images, not mere logic-chopping. The Council fathers at Chalcedon had enthusiastically endorsed the analysis of these matters by Leo, Bishop of Rome (440-461), as set forth in the "Tome of Leo," dated 13 June 449. "Peter has spoken through Leo," they said. "This is [also] the teaching of Cyril [of Jerusalem]. Anathema to him who believes otherwise." Let me give you just a few sentences from the Tome on the subject of Christ's virgin birth before we look at the images that the bishops at Chalcedon perfected in expressing Leo's views:

> Thus there was born true God in the entire and perfect nature of true man, complete in his own properties, and complete in ours

102

[*totus in suis, totus in nostris*]. . . . Jesus Christ was born from a virgin's womb, by a miraculous birth. And yet his [human] nature is not on that account unlike to ours, for he that is true God is also true man. . . . Each nature performs its proper functions in communion with the other; the Word performs what pertains to the Word, the flesh what pertains to the flesh.

Now then: on to the imagery in the Chalcedonian Definition.

First, a look at the phrase "in two natures" *(en duo physesin)*. Simply put, the Council fathers carried previous orthodox thought to completion and decided to use the image of nature [*physis*] to describe what Christ had *two* of — namely, humanity and Deity — and the image of substance [*ousia*] to describe his *oneness* with the Father in the Trinity. It's important to remember that there was a certain arbitrariness in this: the precise Christian signification of these words had been a matter of debate for centuries. They were widely used but also variously understood.

What the Council actually did, therefore, was come to an agreement that thenceforth the image of *ousia* ("substance," "essence") would be assigned to the Deity of Christ, thus portraying him as having one and the same being with the Father; and that the image of *hypostasis* ("person," "subsistence") would be assigned to the way he was distinct from the Father within that Deity. This wasn't as easy as it might sound. The fact that Eastern theologians wrote in Greek and Western ones in Latin complicated the matter. Take the confusion over *ousia* and *hypostasis*, for example. The usual Latin translation of *ousia* was either *essentia* or *substantia* (as it is in English: "essence" or "substance"). But the Christian Latinists rendered *hypostasis* as *persona*, even though, by etymology, *hypostasis* could just as easily mean "substance." (*Sub-stantia* in Latin means "that which stands under" something, its essential, underlying being; and *hypostasis* in Greek has the very same etymology.)

This already confusing situation was further complicated by the fact that while *persona* was a suitable image for translating *hypostasis* in the West, the parallel word in Greek failed to pass muster. *Dramatis personae* in Latin meant "the persons [masks, roles, characters] of a play"; the parallel phrase in Greek was *ta prosōpa tou dramatos*. But even though *prosōpa* too meant "characters," it had been ruined as an orthodox image in the East ever since its use by certain heretics (Sabellians) who claimed that there was really only one Divine Actor: a non-Trinitarian God who simply put on *prosōpa*, or masks, in revealing himself as Father, Son, and Spirit. In any case, here is a chart that might help you remember the names and numbers of all the players in this particular game of images:

The Son of God as he is
WITHIN THE TRINITY

The Son is IDENTICAL with the Father in	SUBSTANCE, *ousia, substantia* ESSENCE, *ousia, essentia* and NATURE, *physis, natura*
The Son is DISTINCT from the Father in	PERSON, *hypostasis, persona, subsistentia*

The Son of God as he is
INCARNATE IN OUR Lord JESUS CHRIST

In his *humanity*, Christ has TWO	NATURES, *physeis, naturae*, one Divine, the other human
But *both* of those natures coexist in only ONE	PERSON, *hypostasis, persona*, namely, the Person of the Word of God

To give you just one more "study help," here's a two-sentence summary of the whole matter: In the *Trinity*, there is one *Whatness* (Deity) and three *Whos* (three Persons: the Father, the Son, and the Holy Spirit). But in the *Incarnation*, there are two *whatnesses* (Deity and humanity) and one *Who* (the Person of the Son).

Even that brief memory aid may strike you as no clearer than mud. But it does so only if you try to take it as propositional theology, as definition by way of logical architecture. On the other hand, if you look at it through the logic of images — as the assignment of specific word-pictures to specific mysteries — it begins to light up. Its apparent complexity dissolves into the simplicity of an agreement to see these images as snapshots of God in Christ: as a photo album that on some pages displays the Word as he is in relationship to God the Father, and on others shows the Word as Incarnate in Jesus. And that's because nouns, adjectives, verbs, and adverbs don't have to be taken simply as concepts for grasping physical reality; they can often be seen as images, metaphors, or types that enable us to grapple with mystery. Indeed, this is the principal way the Hebrew Scriptures use them. In the Old Testament, *lamb* is far more than just an animal. It graduates early on into being one of the principal images of the Bible: it becomes an emblem of deliverance from the death of Egypt's firstborn, and of festal community during the Passover meal, and finally of absolution in the sacrifices of the Temple. And in the New Testament, this elevation continues until *lamb* becomes the image that carries the story to completion. John calls Jesus the Lamb of God who takes away the sin of the world, and Revelation presents the Incarnate Word as the Lamb who turns into the Bridegroom whose Bride is the Holy City, the New Jerusalem, the New Creation.

Watch how this conversion of words into images functions in the four "without" phrases with which the Definition of Chalcedon asserts the mysteries of the Trinity and the Incarnation. In Greek, "without" is expressed by putting what's called an alpha privitive (an *a-* prefix, equivalent to the English *un-*) on any given word. Thus *a-chōristos,* "without separation," conjures up not just the image of separation as such but all the associated images of marital separation, divorce, and the general breakdown of oneness. These alpha privitives even come into our own vocabulary when English forms words with Greek roots: *a*-moral, *a*-typical, *a*-morphous, *an*-orexic (without *desire* for food), and so on.

First then, *a-sygchytos,* "without confusion" — which summons up all the images of *blending, mixture,* and *mix-up.* This word picture was directed against the Apollinarian image of Christ as Clark Kent. It gives us an image not of a human nature that was gussied up by its union with the Divine Word but of a humanity which he assumed in full and as such. It was also a slap at Eutyches's theandric, single-natured Christ — a Christ who wasn't both true God and complete man but a jumbled-up, freakish being who was ultimately irrelevant to our humanity.

Second, *a-treptōs,* "without change" — which invokes the images of *alteration, slippage,* and *alienation* and applies them to *nature* seen as the "birthright," the "inheritance," the "natural property" of a given creature. This word was designed to set aside all the doctrines and resulting images of the Incarnation in which Christ's Deity was tampered with in order to make it compatible with his humanity — Adoptionism, for example, which said that Jesus wasn't really God but just an available human being who had been "adopted" by the Father; or Apollinarianism and Eutychianism, which held that his authentic humanity had been overpowered by his Divinity. It said that Christ had *two* unchanged natures. His Godhead was 100 percent God, without a scrap of humanity in it; and his humanity was 100 percent human, without a scrap of Deity in it. Each was utterly true to its own nature, completely itself and none other; and yet each was perfectly one with the other in the Person of the Word of God.

Next *a-diairetōs,* "without division" — which took the image of *person* with all its freight of *identity,* of *selfhood,* of *who* we are, and made it sit still to give a picture of the one Christ, the one Self, the one Person who speaks to us in Jesus. And in Christ, that Person was the Person of the Word of God, the Divine Son. This is perhaps the most difficult of the Chalcedonian images for us to appreciate. That's because we now confuse *person* with *personality,* at least in the popular imagination. Admittedly, we still have available to us the legal image of person, by which we go on being "selves" in the eyes of the law no matter how we behave or change — even if we end up like vegetables on life support and have no "personality" at all. This image predates our concept of personality by several millennia; and it still survives in the respect given to a person's last will and testament. John Smith, even dead as a doornail, goes right on being the only effective disposer of what was his. Accordingly, if you apply that older image of *person* to Christ as the Council of Chalcedon imaged him, there's no possibility of splitting him into two persons, one Divine and the other human. Who He Is remains the same throughout his career. Before the beginning or at the creation; infant or adult on earth; alive, dead, risen, ascended, in the Eucharist, or at the end of time — whenever or wherever anyone meets him, that person meets the Person of the Word.

"Personality," however, simply can't give you a picture like that. It's true that Jesus of Nazareth (the Jesus who confronts us on the pages of the New Testament) can be said to have a human personality — that is, to have individual characteristics that distinguish him from other human beings — characteristics like tricks of speech, cleverness in argument, and a knack for annoying the hell out of his adversaries. But those traits were simply unique expressions of the everyday human nature he shared with the rest of us. Even the God of the Old Testament had much the same "personality." But in any case, that wasn't what the Council had in mind. They wanted to say that if Christ really was the Word of God Incarnate, then the most important thing they had to decide about him was not "Do we like or dislike the cut of his jib?" but "Do we know Who he really is?" — and above all, "Is Who He Is actually one Person or a committee of two?" And their answer to the last question was "One absolutely! One Person *adiairetōs!* No division at all!"

Finally, *a-chōristōs,* "without separation" — without any wedges being driven between the *two natures* of Christ, without any estrangement shipwrecking their perfect union. This image goes beyond simply refusing to view Jesus as a committee. It says that his human nature, though radically other than his Divine nature, never once had a single argument with it — that his humanity was always in agreement with his heavenly Father; that he always was, and always is, one Christ. It's a rebuke to the perennial nonsense which tries to say that maybe, just to make Jesus more like us, we should be willing to see him as a sinner. I'll give you a little wiggle room on that one, since the doctrine of the sinlessness of Christ has led some people to turn him into either Little Lord Fauntleroy or Superman. Now it's certainly true that many of the characters who ran into Jesus on the street (Scribes and Pharisees, Inc., to cite one example) never thought of him as an example of perfection. They found him a very bad egg indeed, and they even had him executed for the sin of blasphemy.

But I give you no more room than that. Sin is not a part of human nature, let alone a necessary part. It's an accident of our humanity, a moving violation that we can't keep ourselves from committing. But since sin was totally absent from the human race when the Word of God first created it, there was no alternative but for sin to be just as absent when that same Word revealed its re-creation by his Incarnation in our Lord Jesus Christ. And that's because his word about us, first or last, is the word that has a bark to it: what he says is what we are. Anything we ever say to the contrary, at whatever length or however loudly, just doesn't count. Once again, God "made him who knew no sin to become sin for us that we might become the righteousness of God in him." Therefore, as the Council imaged the matter, the whole point of the Incarnation of the Word was to restore us to what we truly are — to recapitulate our nature as what it had been all along in him — so that the beauty of the image of the Word in which we were created might shine forth again in the fullness of its glory. In the eyes of the Council fathers, separating his humanity from his Divinity by making him a seriously bad boy could only make hash of the entire project.

But at last, enough. Time for the next skip of my history-skimming stone: a look at how the doctrine of the Atonement, despite all this prodigious image-crafting, managed to get its nose into the tent of Incarnation and very nearly topple it.

SIX

The Camel in the Tent

The early writers we've touched on so far weren't as preoccupied with the notion of Atonement as later theologians came to be. Admittedly, they often tried to explain *why* it was that Jesus alone could be the Savior of the world; but they stayed away from giving any lesser reason for the effectiveness of his "work" than the fact that he was God the Word himself, Incarnate in our flesh. The author of Hebrews, for example, may have tracked the Divine Suspect through the imagery of the Old Testament sacrificial system which he applied to Jesus' death on the cross. But his delight in its stunning correspondences with that death kept him well clear of subjugating the Atonement to a "job description" of actions that Jesus had to take in order to bring it off. He was thrilled by his discovery that blood and sacrifice and priesthood were images which could be applied to the Person of Jesus; but he never seriously advanced the idea that they should be seen as operational gadgets that could be effective in and of themselves.

For another instance of the same reluctance to explain Jesus' status by requirements he satisfied rather than by the Person he was, consider Irenaeus once again. He held fast to his often-repeated insistence that our restoration is accomplished by the recapitulation of our entire history in the Person of the Word. Here's a glimpse of his approach, from *Against the Heresies,* II iv, 4:

He came to save all through himself; all, that is, who through him are born of God, infants, children, boys, young men, and old. Therefore he passed through every stage of life: he was made an infant for infants, sanctifying infancy; a child among children, sanctifying those of that age . . . a young man amongst young men, . . . sanctifying them to the Lord. So also amongst the older men; that he might be a perfect master for all, not solely in regard to the revelation of truth, but also in respect of each stage of life. And then he came even unto death that he might be "the firstborn from the dead, holding the pre-eminence among all" [Col. 1:18], the Prince of Life, before all and preceding all.

You've no doubt noticed that the fathers of the church, in addition to not having read Fowler's *Modern English Usage,* were born too soon to have a guilty conscience about using only masculine nouns when referring to human nature. "Boys, young men, and old men," they thought, covered that ground nicely. Sadly, they never entertained the notion of *mothers* of the church.

All the same, Irenaeus's insistence on the mystery of the Word Incarnate in Person has been remarkably well preserved by the church. In the Great Litany of the Book of Common Prayer, for example, it shines forth brilliantly. Let me cite the relevant portion for you from one of the older versions:

By the mystery of thy holy Incarnation; by thy holy Nativity
and Circumcision; by thy Baptism, Fasting, and Temptation,
Good Lord, deliver us.

By thine Agony and Bloody Sweat; by thy Cross and Burial;
by thy glorious Resurrection and Ascension; and by the
Coming of the Holy Ghost,
Good Lord, deliver us.

In all time of our tribulation; in all time of our prosperity;
in the hour of death, and in the day of Judgment,
Good Lord, deliver us.

110

Note how well this echoes what I've previously said about the events of Christ's life as mysteries rather than transactions. The Litany shows us Jesus as *being* the Redeemer, not as *doing* redemptive stuff. He's the Savior of the world in his Incarnation, pure and simple: his mere, hidden presence in Mary's womb delivers us, not something he did later. In his Birth all our births are recapitulated, and in his Circumcision the whole world has been made Jewish. (I understand why the 1979 revision of the Prayer Book substituted "submission to the Law" for "Circumcision": "circumcision" was felt to be too exclusively male, or perhaps even too coarse. But I still don't like the replacement. The original word was carrying freight I'm not willing to jettison: the image of an old covenant made in blood, the image of the New Covenant in Jesus' blood, and above all, the image of a "circumcision not made with hands" in Colossians — all of those are too precious to fiddle with. One of my cavils with politically correct revisers of ancient texts is that in their haste to make Scripture relevant to the present, they tear down landmark images which the city of the church's discourse can ill afford to lose.)

But back to the Litany. In Jesus' Baptism, every creature is baptized; in his Fasting and Temptation, all the hunger and all the "testing" of the human race is summed up; in his Agony and Bloody Sweat, all our anguish is present, just as it is in his Cross and Passion; in his Death and Burial, everyone's long home is held forever; in his Resurrection, all humanity rises; in his Ascension, we all go to the Father; and in the Coming of the Holy Ghost, the Spirit comes upon every child of Adam and Eve. But best of all, the Litany triumphantly gives us the same comfort in its last paragraph: it shifts to what is *ours*. It says that in our tribulations, in our prosperity, in our deaths, and in the judgment that's finally pronounced over every one of us, the Word Incarnate, with all his mercy and grace, is there for us no matter what the changes and chances of this life may bring.

It's still Athanasius, though, who best exemplifies the early fathers' contention that it isn't what Christ does that saves us but Who He Is. To refresh your grip on his insight, let me retranslate just two sentences I've already quoted from his *De Incarnatione* (VII, 4):

But once the transgression [of the human race] had gotten the upper hand, so that men were held in bondage to natural decay and had lost the grace they had by being in the image [of the Word], what else needed to happen? Or to put the matter more correctly, of Whom was there need for such a grace and recalling but of the Word of God who at the beginning had made everything from nothing?

Those words are another proof of the patristic preference for arguing from the image of the Person of Christ rather than from his job requirements. Athanasius gives a wide berth to the notion of Jesus' Atonement as a "task" — a "what" that he accomplished by fulfilling a transactional bill of particulars — and he rests his case for the effectiveness of Christ's reconciling grace entirely and only on his status as God the Word by whom all things were made — on the "Who" that he is.

To this point, then, the patristic views of what happened in the death of Jesus could hardly be called theories of the Atonement. They had kept all such hitchhiking job descriptions firmly belted in the back seat of an incarnational automobile whose only Driver was the Word of God himself. But their successors couldn't keep up that admirable arrangement. In the succeeding centuries, one of those back-seat passengers in particular began clamoring for front-seat status. This pain in the neck was the "ransom" view of the Atonement, which held that the death of Jesus saves the world because it's literally a transaction between God and the devil — a bit of bargaining by which God springs us from bondage to Satan by paying off the old deceiver. In fairness to the better minds of the time, I should note that this crude notion of a "payoff" to the prince of darkness was rejected by many of them. Gregory of Nazianzus, for example, ranted against it. "Was [this ransom] paid to the evil one?" he asked. "Monstrous thought! [That would mean that] the devil receives a ransom not only *from* God but *of* God! Was it paid to the Father? But we were not in bondage to him. . . . And could the Father delight in the death of his Son?"

There was, however, another version of the transaction-with-the-devil view that wasn't nearly as dreadful, and which was truer to the logic of images. This one took off from the image of *bait* and portrayed the devil as pouncing on it. It still depicted God as doing a kind of deal with the father of lies; but in a stroke of brilliance, it imaged that deal as a crafty fraud on the part of God — a bit of trickery by which he didn't even give the devil a sporting chance. Consider the version of that which Rufinus of Aquileia (around 400) included in his *Commentary on the Apostolic Symbol* (14ff.):

> The purpose of the Incarnation . . . was that the divine virtue of the Son of God might be as it were a hook hidden beneath the form of human flesh . . . to lure the prince of this age to a contest; [so] that the Son might offer him his flesh as a bait and that then the Divinity which lay beneath might catch him and hold him fast with its hook . . . so he that had the power of death seized the body of Jesus in death, unaware of the hook of Divinity concealed therein. Having swallowed it, he was caught straightway: the bars of hell were burst, and he was as it were drawn up from the pit to become food for others.

This is my kind of theology: theology as ironic fun — which is the only kind that can keep you from turning your images into monstrosities. It's a metaphor of redemption as a bait-and-switch scam perpetrated by God himself. But it was Augustine, the Bishop of Hippo from 396 to 430, who brought this bit of theological whimsy to perfection: *"Crux muscipulum diaboli,"* he said in a marvelous sermon: "The cross is a mousetrap set for the devil." And then, almost like a stand-up comic, he went on to milk the image for all it was worth. The devil looks into the "box-and-stick" trap of Calvary and licks his lips over the prospect of feasting on the bait of the Son of God's death. He enters the trap and takes the bait. His move on the bait pulls the string attached to the stick, and the box falls down with the devil trapped inside. But then, in one of the great homiletical clinchers of all time, Augustine comes up with the punch line: *The bait turns out to be fake!* Christ refuses to stay dead and springs the whole world by the power of his resurrection!

Unfortunately, lesser and grimmer minds had little talent for this sort of patristic larking around. All they could do was propositionalize their own brand of theological hell back into it — complete with a God who actually owed the devil his due and who was required by some metaphysical necessity to pay off the infernal Mafia with the death of his only Son. Obviously, that image of redemption by paying blackmail wasn't just grim and blasphemous; it was downright wrong. Rufinus, Gregory, and Augustine may have been a tribute to how right the church can be at its playful best. But these later minds were equally a tribute to how much nonsense the church can spout when it loses its sense of humor — and to how long it can keep on spouting it. From the fifth century to the eleventh, the Ransom Theory (often in its crassest forms) was practically the church's official view of the Atonement.

I want to say, "Shades of the cart before the Horse," but that's not the half of it. This was twenty tons of concrete slabbing that the Horse had to pull uphill for six hundred years! So let's bypass that time of cruel and unusual punishment and go straight to Anselm, Archbishop of Canterbury — perhaps the greatest Western theologian from Augustine to Aquinas.

❧

First, a brief *curriculum vitae* of this extraordinary man. Anselm was born to noble parents at Aosta in the Piedmont region of Italy in the year 1033. He received a classical education and was soon recognized for his precise intellect and for the elegance of his Latin style. He became a monk of the Benedictine abbey of Bec in Normandy in 1060; and he rapidly advanced to the positions of prior (in 1063) and abbot (in 1078). After the abbey had been given a gift of lands in Normandy and England by William I (the Conqueror), Anselm made three visits to the abbey's English holdings. When he founded the abbey of Chester, he was named Archbishop of Canterbury by William II. But he refused consecration to the post until that second William (a royal troublemaker) consented to recognize Urban II as the legitimate pope, and undertook to restore the Canterbury lands he had seized. Anselm was finally consecrated Archbishop on 4 December 1093. He died in 1109.

He wrote three principal works. His *Monologion* (1077) was a meditation by reason on the existence and attributes of God. His *Proslogion* (1078) was a treatise in which he set forth the "ontological argument," perhaps his best-known contribution to Christian thought. It was a proof of the existence of God which proceeded from the notion that the very idea of "a Being than whom no greater can be conceived" necessarily contains within itself the notion of existence. Finally, his *Cur Deus Homo?* (1097-99) stands as his monumental work on the Atonement. It's the book that brings the brilliant but eventually seductive image of *satisfaction* into Western theology, and it's the only one I'll be concerned with here.

Accordingly, I'm going to give two longer-than-usual quotations from *Cur Deus Homo?* My purpose in trying your patience this way is partly to give you an idea of the clarity of Anselm's dialectic; but it's mostly to show you how far we've moved from the early fathers in this abrupt skip to the Middle Ages. Trust me, I'm just warming up to the heart of my argument for what went wrong with medieval theology — and to what the Reformers never quite spotted as being a false start. (Just one preliminary comment. Literally, the book's title translates as *Why God Man?;* but it might be more accessibly rendered as "Why the God-Man?" or even "Why God Became Man." In any case, here's the first citation, from Book One:

> xi The problem is, how can God forgive man's sin? To clear our thoughts let us first consider what sin is, and what satisfaction for sin is. . . . To sin is to fail to render God his due. What is due to God? Righteousness, or rectitude of will. He who fails to render this honor to God robs God of that which belongs to him, and dishonors God. . . . And what is satisfaction? It is not enough simply to restore what has been taken away; [rather], in consideration of the insult offered, more than what was taken away must be rendered back.
>
> xii Let us consider whether God could properly remit sin by mercy alone without satisfaction. To remit sin in that way would be simply to abstain from punishing it. And since the only possible way of correcting sin for which no satisfaction has been made is to punish it, not to punish it is to remit it uncorrected. But God cannot properly leave anything uncorrected in his king-

dom. Moreover, so to remit sin unpunished would be treating the sinful and the sinless alike, which would be incongruous to God's nature. And incongruity is injustice.

xiii It is necessary, therefore, that either the honor taken away should be repaid, or punishment should be inflicted. Otherwise one of two things follows: either God is not just to himself, or he is powerless to do what he ought to do. A blasphemous supposition. . . .

xxi And you have not yet duly estimated the gravity of sin. Suppose that you were standing in God's presence, and someone said to you, "Look yonder." And God said, "I am altogether unwilling that you should look." Ask yourself whether there is anything in the whole creation for the sake of which you should indulge that one look against the will of God. Not [even] to preserve the whole creation from perishing should you act against the will of God. And if you should so act, what can you pay for this sin? You cannot make satisfaction for it unless you pay something greater than the whole creation. All that is created (that is, all that is not God) cannot compensate the sin.

Note first that Anselm has made a significant shift in emphasis here. He's left the notion of a debt owed to the devil far behind and rested his view of the Atonement on the image of a satisfaction due to God. So much so, that his view of the Atonement has come to be called the Satisfaction Theory. As such, it became the church's principal way of understanding that mystery not only throughout the Middle Ages but also during the Reformation era and far beyond it. In fact, it's been only in the last century or so that widespread questions about it have been raised.

Note too, however, that satisfaction did not turn out to be as good an image for Christ's Atonement as Anselm thought it was. For centuries before his time, the notions of reparation, recompense, and restitution had been taking command of legal thinking about crime. And, by a theological extension, those same "requirements" had increasingly been applied to *sin*. But to put requirements on God's forgiveness is not a good idea — and it's certainly a major departure from Irenaeus, Athanasius, and their friends. For those theologians, it was the Incarnate Word's *relationship* with the Father that was the "cause" of redemption: the entire business of reconciliation was accomplished simply because Christ was the Father's beloved Son, not because of things the Son did to set matters right with the First Person of the Trinity. Admittedly, when Anselm applied the image of satisfaction to the Person of the Incarnate Word, he did so because he thought that only an infinite Person could make up for an infinite offense. But the merely plausible notion of making amends was still a poor image for the mystery by which we're reconciled. Images have the power to corrupt as well as to edify — and bad images have the power to corrupt absolutely.

Because once you've let the cat of satisfaction out of the bag, it produces nasty kittens right and left. And first among them is *punishment*, a tough little ball of fur that has an inbred hostility to forgiveness. In Paul and his successors, forgiveness is always a free gift, not something the sinner has to earn by offering satisfaction for his or her dereliction. But as soon as this kitten grows up, it tries to turn satisfaction into the *condition* of forgiveness. It was this subjugation of forgiveness to something less than the mystery of love between the Persons of the Trinity that was Anselm's grim legacy to subsequent ages. Soon enough, it led the church to assume that "making up for sin" was a necessary ingredient for the soup of pardon — and that without it, God couldn't forgive the world. (It makes no difference, by the way, whether you assign this making up solely to Christ or think of it as something human beings have to do on their own. Once you put the requirement of sufficient recompense on God, you hang a sign that says "No Satisfaction, No Forgiveness" in the front window of the Divine Store.)

This limitation on God's (or anybody else's) freedom to absolve misdeeds has survived to the present day in the legal concept of "punitive damages": a person harmed by another is allowed not only to seek compensation for the injury itself but also to sue for the "pain and suffering" caused by it. But this permission to seek reparation for injured dignity also survives in the popular imagination, where it's been elevated almost to the status of a commandment. Even now, after two millennia of the Gospel message that forgiveness is an unmerited gift dependent only on the arbitrary goodness of the giver, we commonly suppose that no one should be forgiven unless he or she is sufficiently sorry for the sin committed. The reaction of many people to President Clinton's sexual affair was that he hadn't "done enough" to warrant absolution for his dalliance with Monica Lewinsky. Even his perfectly legal challenges to his accusers' tactics were seen as evidence of insufficient penitence — and therefore as proof that he was unworthy of forgiveness.

Moreover, in the cases of less prominently placed sinners, the common view is that any sin serious enough to cause irreparable injury is simply unpardonable. The dishonored wife of the adulterer concludes that her suffering is such that no reparations on his part can make up for it. The family of the murdered daughter feels perfectly entitled to tell the press that no repentance by the murderer counts at all in their minds, because their grief over the girl's death can't be compensated for by anything short of bringing her back to life. (Their clamor for capital punishment is irrelevant: her killer's death couldn't revive her any more than his repentance would.) In short, the image of sufficient satisfaction encourages the worst in human nature. It deludes us into thinking we can follow the God who forgave us from the low horse of the cross by getting up on the high horse of our pain and suffering and refusing to forgive.

But that's all pure, anti-Gospel nonsense. For example. Every time we say the Lord's Prayer ("forgive us *as* we forgive"), Jesus reminds us that the only unforgivable sin is the sin *we decide* not to forgive. So it's not sin that fouls up our enjoyment of God's forgiveness; it's our refusal to pass that forgiveness along to others. If the Lamb of God has already taken away the sins of the world, how can we ignore that gift when it's our turn to give it? The answer, alas, is all too readily — but only at the price of going against the grain of God's new creation. Still, like all the yokes and burdens Jesus lays on us, this passing along of forgiveness is both easy and light. If I choose to drop the subject of someone's trespasses against me, who's to say I can't, except me? If God wants to extend mercy, his justice doesn't seem to forbid him. So who am I to harp on satisfaction before I forgive my brother-in-law?

Accordingly, if God the Father wants to forgive the world simply because he sees it through the lens of his beloved Son, who's to tell him he mustn't? Are we to tell him he's being foolish and weak? Paul long ago put that gambit out of reach by declaring that we're saved precisely by the foolishness and weakness of God (1 Cor. 1:18-25). Are we to turn our backs on that and advise God that he has to respect his own dignity and forgive only sinners who can offer a sufficient apology for their insult to him? Preposterous thought! God in Christ embraced our insult to his dignity: "No one takes my life from me; I lay it down *of myself*" (John 10:18; italics mine).

But I'll be quiet and let Anselm continue his case, this time from Book II of *Cur Deus Homo?*:

> iv It is necessary that God should fulfill his purpose respecting human nature. And this cannot be except there be a complete *satisfaction* made for sin: and this, no sinner can make. . . .
>
> vi Satisfaction cannot be made unless there be some One able to pay to God for man's sin something greater than all that is beside God. . . . Now nothing is greater than all that is not God except God himself. None therefore can make this satisfaction except God. And none ought to make it except man. . . . If then it is necessary that the kingdom of heaven be completed by man's admission, and if man cannot be admitted unless the aforesaid satisfaction for sin be first made, and if God alone can and man alone ought to make this satisfaction, then necessarily One must make it who is both God and man. . . .
>
> xi Now [that One] must have something to offer greater than all that is below God, and something that he can give to God voluntarily and not as in duty bound. Mere obedience would not be a gift of this kind; for every rational creature owes this obedience as a duty to God. But death, Christ was in no way bound to suffer, having never sinned. So death was an offering he could make as of free will, and not of debt. . . .
>
> xix Now One who could freely offer so great a gift to God clearly ought not to be without reward. . . . But what reward could be given to One who needed nothing — One who craved neither gift nor pardon? . . . [But] if the Son chose to make over the claim he had on God to man, could the Father justly forbid him doing so, or refuse to man what the Son willed to give him?

xx What greater mercy can be conceived than that God the Father should say to the sinner [who is] condemned to eternal torment and unable to redeem himself, "Receive my only Son, and offer him for yourself"; while the Son himself said, "Take me, and redeem yourself"? And what greater justice [could there be] than that One [the Father] who receives [such] a payment far exceeding the amount due should, if it be paid with the right intention, remit all that is due?

True enough, in both of the passages I've cited from Anselm, he does manage to imply that the satisfaction he was talking about was made by God (the Son) to God (the Father) — thus making the Atonement an "effect" of the Son alone and keeping it in the bosom of the Trinity. On any fair reading, the whole "process" remains strictly God's business. Nevertheless, Anselm's mother cat of satisfaction still found a way to give the kitten of requirement a home in the Trinitarian household. And that little beast spent the rest of its long career tempting the church to dream up reasons why God *had to* act the way he did — when all along the church should have been encouraging itself simply to admire the mystery of what the Father did for no reason whatsoever other than his delight in his Son.

The church should never have allowed the images that Anselm set before it to dominate its thinking. Consider *condemned to eternal torment,* for example. No doubt that's a fair description of how refusal of God's forgiveness can make us feel; and it's certainly a fate that Jesus wasn't afraid to talk about. And if we try to resist his forgiveness forever, it will be hell enough for anybody. But it's a damned poor way of setting up a doctrine of the Atonement. For one thing, it runs clean contrary to Paul in Romans 8:1: "There is therefore now no condemnation for those who are in Christ Jesus." Furthermore, if you have even the least inkling of Who Christ Is (namely, the Word of God who holds all things, even hell, in being by his speaking), there's no way you can put anything, even hell, outside him. No one can escape the presence of the creating and atoning Word, and no one can lose the effectiveness of his power. You may resist it beyond the clap of doom. But resist as you will, *you,* at the roots of your being in him, will be forever uncondemned.

Equally dangerous, though, are two more images contained in the final paragraphg I quoted from Anselm (xx, above). "*Take me, and redeem yourself*" can of course be given a benign interpretation and read as "*Trust me, and you will find yourself already redeemed.*" That would make it consistent with the assertion in Ephesians and Colossians that the whole world was *in Christ* even before anyone believed in him. It would agree with what the author of Ephesians was getting at when he held that the Gentiles (the entire non-Jewish creation) were *in Christ* from the beginning: "But now in Christ Jesus you who were once far off have been made near *by the blood of Christ*" (2:13; italics mine). And it would also be consonant with Colossians 2:13, where the author states that the Gentiles had been made the chosen people of God by the mystery of Christ's own circumcision. He doesn't say that their faith made that mystery a reality for them; he just presents them with the mystery of what they'd long since become in Christ, and he invites them to trust Christ. But the words *take me* inevitably give the impression that anyone who doesn't take him (who refuses to "accept Christ") doesn't have him yet — thus giving rise to all the bad theology that automatically consigned Jews, Turks, and infidels to hell. And the phrase *redeem yourself* is even worse. It suggests that when push comes to shove, redemption is our responsibility. To be sure, without faith we will never enjoy our existence in the Beloved. But even with no faith on our part, our perpetual *being* in Christ goes right on. Paul did indeed command the Philippians (in 2:12) to "work out your own salvation with fear and trembling"; but he followed that up (in 2:13) with this truly operational phrase: "because it is *God* who works in you, both to will and to do his good pleasure."

Anselm, I'm sure, wasn't ignorant of that better image; perhaps he even had it in mind when he came up with those last two phrases. Still, since Scripture has other images that might have taken the curse of atonement-by-self-help off his argument, I think he would have done better to weave one or two of them into it. One such image might have been the Psalmist's *River of love* I mentioned earlier. That's a picture of the torrent of forgiveness by which the whole world is being borne into the joy of God. By comparison, theological explanations of how the river carries us home don't even amount to a trickle. But the best image of all might still have been the old one from Irenaeus and Athanasius: the image of the Son doing *nothing new* in his Incarnation — not even when he made Atonement. That's a picture of the Word just being who he has been from the beginning: the eternal Son who is always creating us in his image and conferring upon us his likeness — before, during, or after sin. Had Anselm hung that image more prominently in the church's mental portrait gallery, we might have been spared many centuries of either bad taste in images or no taste at all.

But that's the last bone I intend to pick with Anselm. On to a guided tour of the sometimes grim museum we've had to put up with since the Reformers and their successors took over its artistic direction.

SEVEN

A Chat in the Museum of Images

For me, writing a book has always been an exercise in juggling images. My custom is to accumulate a deskful of them in the course of my preaching, lecturing, and random rumination and then try to turn them into something presentable. But metaphors sitting in the mind do not a book make; they're just a basket of wash that not even I (let alone anyone else) can see as a coherent whole. Long ago, therefore, I developed an image for what I do as an author. When I write, I see myself as hanging theological laundry on a clothesline: until I can find the right rope to pin my wash to, no book is possible. To be sure, there's always a story to be read in anybody's laundry (your neighbor's unmentionables on the line can tell you volumes about her style and substance); but if the clothes just stay in the basket, the story can neither edify nor titillate.

I tell you this because this book is an attempt to deal with some three or four years' worth of theological shirts, socks, and underwear that have been daring me to get them hung out intelligibly. Over a year ago, I started to write them up under the title of *Re-forming the Reformation*. My hope at the time was that if I could display them on the line of "medieval abuses the Reformers left unreformed," that would do the job. I could begin with a bow to the Reformers' success in correcting the abuses they did spot (salvation by works, for instance, as opposed to salvation by grace) and then proceed to what I saw as their failure to spot a host of other abuses (propositionalism, transactionalism, confusion between faith and *the* faith) — and above all, their leftover medieval habit of assigning the effectiveness of Christ's salvation to things he did or said rather than to Who He Is. After that, I thought I'd follow the history of those failures right up to the present and conclude with my thesis that only now, after five hundred years of post-Reformation stand-offs, are we finally in a position to make a theological end run around them.

However, as I struggled to hang those items on that clothesline, it slowly dawned on me that the rope was too short. First, it didn't reach far enough to take me back to my newest love: the patristic period with which I've regaled you for the last two chapters. But, in addition, at least some of the half-washed or even unwashed laundry that the Reformers proudly displayed in their yard predated the Reformation by as much as fourteen hundred years. For example, the confusion of faith with *the* faith was creeping into Christian thinking as early as some of the later books of the New Testament itself. For another, anti-Semitism (wildly popular during the Middle Ages and still alive and well in Luther and others) had been plaguing the church's mind since the middle of the second century, if not before. But I've already said a good deal of this, so I'll make a long story short and tell you (if you haven't guessed) what I finally decided to do: I opted for the much longer clothesline I've been using in this book. If you want to count my prologue about the Trinity before creation, consider it an infinitely long rope; but if you prefer to think of it more modestly, let's call it a two-thousand-year line on which I've been pinning as much of Scripture and the early fathers as I happen to have in my basket.

In any case, the book as it now stands (or falls) has brought me to the brink of the Reformation, and to the rest of the laundry I want to show you. But I warn you: I'm nowhere near the end of my supply of clothesline. I reserve the right to extend it as far into the future as I have into the past — just for the fun of ending up, as we believe the world itself will, where we all started from.

124

By the time the Reformation began, a host of abuses had crept into the medieval Western church. To set the stage for what I'm about to do, let me give you a list of just a few of them:

1. The popes' assertions of the supremacy of their spiritual power over the merely temporal power of Christian rulers. The Reformers maintained that such a supremacy couldn't exist because all Christians were declared to be kings and priests at their baptism, and therefore any Christian, if need be, could exercise power not only over secular affairs but over ecclesiastical ones as well. This reform, though, came at the same time as the birth of the nation-states of Europe, and many of the newly minted kings, princes, electors, and margraves were only too glad to take advantage of it for their own political purposes.

2. The church's reliance on fear of hell and eternal torment as inducements to meritorious works — which, it was thought, could spare people such a fate. The Reformers tried to counter this by holding that only faith, not human good works, was "necessary for salvation." But that last phrase was a sleepwalker that came back to haunt even the reformed churches that relied on it.

3. The transactionalizing of salvation, which was the direct result of 2, above. The Reformers always felt they had corrected this abuse with their insistence on salvation by grace through faith; but as I think you'll see, they didn't sufficiently guard against the human race's love of merit and its proclivity for turning faith itself into a kind of "instrument" of salvation — despite the fact that grace can't put up with such an unfortunate description of a personal relationship without altogether ceasing to be grace.

4. The corruption of the sacraments: the medieval church had transformed them from signs of faith and real presences of the grace extended once for all in Christ, and turned them into literal repetitions of his sacrifice — making the Eucharist, for example, a sacrifice in its own right that could be offered here and now for persons living or dead. The Reformers rejected this one outright, holding that while the sacraments were indeed signs and presences of Christ's redemption, their "effectiveness" depended only on faith in the *one sacrifice* that couldn't possibly need repeating.

5. The Middle Age's bad habit of making grace conditional upon meritorious human works, such as the "sacrifices of Masses," pilgrimages, fasts, celibacy, and monastic vows. The Reformers refused to make anything but faith the right response to grace — it was received, they said, *sola fide*. But again, the notion of putting any condition, even faith, on God's free gift in Christ would continue to plague their successors.

6. Finally, there was the medieval church's failure to see Holy Scripture as the ultimate source of authority, plus its general ignorance of the languages in which the Bible was written. The Reformers countered the first of these by adding the watchword *sola Scriptura* to *sola fide:* the church, they said, could never require anything that couldn't be established by the "sure warrant of Scripture"; and they remedied the second by championing the production of vernacular translations from the original Hebrew and Greek.

That's by no means a complete or even an orderly summary of their responses to the abuses they perceived. But perhaps it will do to get us to what I have in mind to give you next: a "conversation" between a few Reformers and myself in which I'll try to challenge them on some of the errors they either incompletely corrected or didn't correct at all. On with a prelude to the conversation.

～

Thomas Aquinas once wrote a commentary on the Gospels that goes by the name of *Catena Aurea,* "The Golden Chain." In it, he took selected passages from a number of church fathers and set them out as a "round table discussion" of the Gospel texts. It's as if he magically reconvened such writers as Origen (d. 253), Hilary of Poitiers (d. 368), Ambrose of Milan (d. 397), John Chrysostom (d. 407), Jerome (d. 420), Augustine (d. 430), Gregory the Great (d. 604), John Damascene (d. 749), Alcuin (d. 804), and many others — possibly including Thomas himself — for a chat with each other about their recognitions of the fingerprints of God in Scripture.

That conversational format was what gave me the idea of presenting the Reformers to you by means of a dialogue. But it will not be a dialogue set in the past that produced our differences. I propose to have it take place in our final resting place — in the Heavenly City itself, long after our disagreements about Christ have been resolved in Christ. My less-than-golden chain may not extend as deeply into the nooks and crannies of our topics as Thomas's did into his; but at least it will reach the matters I've chosen for consideration on that eternal afternoon. So to set what I hope will be the tone of our discussion, let me quote some stanzas from one of my favorite hymns: a ballad of the New Jerusalem by an author known only as F.B.P., and composed, most likely, somewhere between 1571 and 1603:

1 Jerusalem, my happy home,
   When shall I come to thee?
   When shall my sorrows have an end,
   Thy joys when shall I see?

2 O happy harbor of the Saints!
   O sweet and pleasant soil!
   In thee no sorrow may be found,
   No grief, no care, no toil.

4 No dampish mist is seen in thee,
   No cold nor darksome night;
   There every soul shines as the sun,
   There God himself gives light.

5 There lust and lucre cannot dwell;
   There envy bears no sway;
   There is no hunger, heat, nor cold,
   But pleasure every way.

6 Jerusalem, Jerusalem,
   God grant that I may see
   Thy endless joys, and of the same
   Partaker ay may be!

8 Thy turrets and thy pinnacles
   With carbuncles do shine;
   Thy very streets are paved with gold,
   Surpassing clear and fine.

9 Thy houses are of ivory,
   Thy windows Christale clear;
   Thy tiles are made of beaten gold —
   O God that I were there!

13 We that are here in banishment,
   Continually do mourn;
   We sigh and sob, we weep and wail,
   Perpetually we groan.

14 Our sweet is mixed with bitter gall,
   Our pleasure is but pain,
   Our joys scarce last the looking on,
   Our sorrows still remain.

15 But there they live in such delight,
   Such pleasure and such play,
   As that to them a thousand years
   Doth seem as yesterday.

16 Thy vineyards and thy orchards are
   Most beautiful and fair,
   Full furnishèd with trees and fruits,
   Most wonderful and rare;

17 Thy gardens and thy gallant walks
   Continually are green;
   There grow such sweet and pleasant flowers
   As nowhere else are seen.

18 There's nectar and ambrosia made,
   There's musk and civet sweet;
   There many a fair and dainty drug
   Is trodden under feet.

19   There cinnamon, there sugar grows,
     There nard and balm abound;
     What tongue can tell, or heart conceive,
     The joys that there are found!

26   Jerusalem, my happy home,
     Would God I were in thee!
     Would God my woes were at an end
     Thy joys that I might see!

There! I think it's finally safe to begin the conversation.

ROBERT: Gentlemen, it's a privilege for me to be here with you in this splendid setting. As burdensome as our disputes may once have been, by the grace of God we're now bravely over them. So in the spirit of that happy issue out of all our afflictions, I've planned two surprises for you. The second will come at the end of our chat: I've brought a bottle of Scotch — the Macallan, 25 years old — to share with you. But the first one will be an even better treat: I've invited a mystery guest to sit in with us. Since the Reformation was pretty much a fight between two boys' clubs (the New Crowd versus the Medievals), I thought it would be helpful to have a woman, a very special friend of mine, in our midst. We men can get the ball moving; but I'll feel free to call on her to bail us out when we begin to fumble. Let's go to it, then. I suggest we start on the relatively easy territory of the pope's claim that he had power to remit sins by his own authority and look at your retorts to that — your admirable insistence that no one can absolve sins except by declaring Christ's forgiveness, given once for all in his death and resurrection. Since Martin here has gotten the credit for kicking this whole game off, why don't we let him go first?

LUTHER: Fair enough. In the sixth of my *Ninety-Five Theses,* I was quite clear on the subject:

The Pope has no power to remit guilt, save by declaring and confirming that it has been remitted by God (or, to be sure, by re-

129

mitting the cases reserved to himself). If he neglected to observe these limitations the guilt would remain.

ROBERT: That's good, Martin. On the positive side, you give the pope (and by extension, all the ministers of the church) not only a declaratory role in pronouncing absolution but also a confirmatory one. If I may echo one of your assertions elsewhere, you hold that ministerial absolutions work not because the ministers themselves are "able" to absolve sins but because their absolutions are sacraments, true presences of the forgiveness of Christ that exists throughout the church. In any case, you did keep the sacrament of Penance as one of the three ordinances you were willing to see as sacraments of the Gospel (unlike some other Reformers, such as my own Anglican forbears, who limited themselves to Baptism and Communion only). But even though you were careful to root all your sacraments in the one baptismal declaration of forgiveness, I'm afraid you and your successors didn't sufficiently distance yourselves from what I've called transactionalism. I agree, of course, that the absolving gift of Christ can be responded to only by faith. But when you say that "guilt would remain" if the pope or anybody else failed in that faith, you seem to imply that the gift of forgiveness remains ungiven until somebody accepts it. In my view, however, all we have to do with any gift is trust the giver enough to unwrap it. By that act of faith, we do indeed learn what the gift is, and we have the joy of living with it. But even without faith, the unopened gift will still be ours forever. Didn't you say something like that in the Augsburg Confession, Philipp?

MELANCHTHON: Yes. When I was talking about Original Sin, I did say, in Article Two,

> Our churches also teach that since the fall of Adam all men who are propagated according to nature are born in sin. That is to say, they are without fear of God, are without trust in God, and are concupiscent. And this disease or vice of origin is truly sin, which even now damns and brings eternal death on those who are not born again through Baptism and the Holy Spirit.

130

But in Articles Four and Five, on Justification and on The Ministry of the Church, I went on to say . . .

ROBERT: Respectfully, Philipp, I'd like to stop you there for a moment. I'll grant you that apart from the grace of Christ's Incarnation, all those nasty consequences you've mentioned (being "without fear of God" and the rest) fall on us full force; and that apart from him we would all be damned. But that the whole human race is somehow devoid of the grace of his sovereign presence as the Word of God, and therefore apart from him, I can't give you. When Jesus is lifted up from the earth, he "draws *all* to himself," not just those who unwrap the gift of grace by faith. It's his drawing that we count on in faith, not our act of faith itself. And therefore when you say that original sin "brings eternal death on those who are not born again through Baptism and the Holy Spirit," you seem not to have moved far enough by half from the medieval error of putting ecclesiastical mediation between us and Christ. Admittedly, you know better than that. You teach us that the sacraments (and, in particular, the sacrament of the body and blood of Christ) are Christ himself, really present in the fullness of his Deity and humanity; and that there is only one mediator between God and man, the man Christ Jesus (1 Tim. 2:5). But in consigning the unbaptized to hell just for being unbaptized — and by implying that the Holy Spirit sent by Jesus may thus have been a gift not to the whole world but to believers alone — you seem not only to have gone back on the universal implications of Pentecost but to have made the church a mediator of Christ rather than a sacramental presence of him. But do go on.

MELANCHTHON: Thank you, Robert. As I was about to say, I was only trying to get mediation by anyone other than Jesus off the table. When I dealt with Justification in Article Four, I think I did that rather nicely:

> Our churches also teach that men cannot be justified before God by their own strength, merits, or works but are freely justified for Christ's sake through faith when they believe that they

131

are received into favor and that their sins are forgiven on account of Christ, who by his death made satisfaction for our sins. This faith God imputes for righteousness in his sight (Romans 3:4).

And in Article Five, I . . .

ROBERT: Close but no cigar, Philipp. You say "freely justified" through faith out of one side of your mouth, but then you take it back with the other. "When they believe that they are received into favor and that their sins are forgiven" may pass muster if you lean hard enough on *are received;* but that previous *when* unfortunately suggests that before we believe, the free justification isn't ours yet — that the gift is just in the mail, as it were, and hasn't quite reached our address. But if the Gospel says that we've already been "received into favor" for no other reason than Jesus' delivery of forgiveness once and for all on the cross, how is saying that our faith gets it to us any better than making the pope's say-so the deciding factor? Furthermore, I'm afraid you're still stuck in the Anselmic trap of satisfaction. You've mired us in the image of justification as something Jesus did as an agent (albeit a Divine Agent) when you should have been liberating us, as Athanasius did, with the image of Who He Is as the Author of all creation. Admittedly, your legal image of imputation takes at least some of the curse off that: it does manage to say that God accounts us righteous in his Beloved Son because when he looks at us, he sees us only as we are in his Beloved Son. However, it falls short of Paul's flat statement that God "made him who knew no sin to be sin for us that we might become the righteousness of God in him." But since you want to continue with Article Five, be my guest.

MELANCHTHON: Thank you again. What I said there was this:

> In order that we may obtain this faith, the ministry of teaching the Gospel and administering the sacraments was instituted. For through the Word and the sacraments, as through instruments, the Holy Spirit is given, and the Holy Spirit produces

132

faith, where and when it pleases God, in those who hear the Gospel. That is to say, it is not on account of our own merits but on account of Christ that God justifies those who believe that they are received into favor for Christ's sake. Galatians 3:14, "That we might receive the promise of the Spirit through faith."

ROBERT: I'm afraid I still have a few problems with that. For one thing, you seem to equate the Word (capital *W*) with the teaching of the Gospel. That's perhaps pardonable as an honor to the Gospel; but it tends to obscure the primary sense of the "Word of God" as one of the names of the Second Person of the Trinity — so much so that when we were back at the beginning of the third millennium, the average Protestant had come to think "the Word" meant the Bible or the sermon, not Jesus himself as the Incarnate Son of God.

And for another thing — your use of "instruments" sends me up the wall. When you say that the Holy Spirit "is given" through preaching and the sacraments, you open the door to the idea that the Spirit hasn't been given *until* those things happen. I always thought you were very big on the notion that the Father and the Son had the Spirit with them from all eternity and that they had sent him into creation from the start.

But, in particular, when you say that the Spirit produces faith *where and when* it pleases God, you open an even more ominous door. You seem to posit a God who, having made faith the condition of his gift given to the whole world, then seems to withhold the possibility of receiving that gift from people in certain places and times. Once again, I assumed you would have been as enthusiastic as I am about 1 Timothy 2:4: "God wills *all men* to be saved and to come to knowledge of the truth." How can you put a "where and when" on that without blowing it out of the water? Your third sentence, though, doesn't bother me a bit: "*are received* into favor for Christ's sake" covers all the right bases.

CALVIN: May I jump in here, Robert? I too have something to say along these lines — though it may not please you any more than what my *confrères* have said. In my *Institutes of the Christian Religion*, I put it this way (Book III, chapter xxi):

No one who wishes to be thought religious dares outright to deny predestination, by which God chooses some for the hope of life, and condemns others to eternal death. But men entangle it with captious quibbles; and especially those who make fore-knowledge the ground of it. We indeed attribute to God both predestination and foreknowledge; but we call it absurd to sub-ordinate one to the other. When we attribute foreknowledge to God we mean that all things have ever been, and eternally re-main, before his eyes; so that to his knowledge nothing is future or past, but all things are present; and present not in the sense that they are reproduced in imagination (as we are aware of past events which are retained in our memory), but present in the sense that he really sees and observes them placed, as it were, be-fore his eyes. And this foreknowledge extends over the whole universe and over every creature. By predestination we mean the eternal decree of God, by which he has decided in his own mind what he wishes to happen in the case of each individual. For all men are not created on an equal footing, but for some eternal life is pre-ordained, for others eternal damnation.

What do you say about that?

ROBERT: John, I have no problems with your insistence on God's *election,* his eternal choosing of us, as the root of human salvation. I'll also grant you *predestination,* if you like, since you got that image right out of Ephesians. (I do wish, though, that you'd expounded it without parking the nasty image of predetermination in the bosom of God himself.) I'll even give you *eternal damnation,* if you like, pro-vided it's set up in the right way. Jesus introduces the subject plainly enough, especially in his Parables of Judgment — and the church, on the whole, hasn't shied away from it. So I for one feel content to leave it as a real possibility for any of us.

However, when I ask myself the question "On what basis does Jesus say that the possibility of hell can become an actuality?" I be-gin to get a different answer from yours. Admittedly, in other places in your writings, you nicely follow Jesus' parables and make faith, not works, the touchstone of eternal life. I agree. The five wise virgins are rewarded precisely for having enough faith in the Bridegroom's choosing of them to stay at his party and meet him. And the five foolish virgins are locked out for not having such faith and leaving before they could greet him. His command to all ten girls was simply to be there till he came, not to handle the lighting effects at his wedding reception. But on your view of pre-destination, we have to go beyond the evidence of the parable and make the Bridegroom's pre-ordination of faith or unfaith the *cause* of the girls' behavior. That not only wrecks the parable as an invitation to faith but also clouds the obvious fact that the only thing the Bridegroom ever predestined for any of the virgins was the honor of being a member of his wedding. In my book, therefore, his final condemnation of the fools — his exasperated "I don't know you" — hardly qualifies as the predetermined eternal counsel of God. It's more like "I just don't understand girls like you; how could you have so little trust in me as to think I cared more for your silly little lamps than for *you?*"

Worse yet, John, your statement that "all men are not created on an equal footing, but for some eternal life is pre-ordained, for others eternal damnation" gives me the willies, especially when I compare it with John 12:32: "I, if I be lifted up from the earth, will draw *all* to myself." In light of that, I just don't buy the idea that the Word of God — who made us all in his image at the beginning, and who draws us all to himself in the end — would suddenly, in the sixteenth century, inspire you to vitiate that whole operation with your version of predestination. I find that I can quite comfortably allow Helen Damnation into my theological imagery without letting her ride so rudely over Jesus' plans for our season.

But rather than belabor such sad matters further, I think it's time to bring on my mystery challenger. I have no idea whether any of you were familiar with her while you were pursuing your careers on earth, but now that all our times are so obviously in God's hands, I'm sure you'll welcome her. She is the Lady Julian of Norwich, the great English mystic and Anchoress, who was born around 1342 and who was still living in 1413. Her book, *Revelations of Divine Love*, was completed before 1393; it stands as one of the brightest candles of the High Middle Ages. Julian?

JULIAN: I'm a simple creature, unlettered, and not at all used to discourse. All I know is what the church taught me and what our Lord himself revealed to me, so forgive me if I seem not to understand your subtleties. I say only what was told me:

> XXXI Thus our good Lord answered to all the questions and doubts I might make, saying full comfortably: *I may make all thing well, I can make all thing well, I will make all thing well, and I shall make all thing well; and thou shalt see thyself that all manner of thing shall be well.* In that He saith, *I may,* I understand [it] for the Father; and in that He saith, *I can,* I understand [it] for the Son; and where He saith, *I will,* I understand [it] for the Holy Ghost; and where He saith, *I shall,* I understand [it] for the unity of the blessed Trinity: three Persons and one Truth; and where he saith, *Thou shalt see thyself,* I understand the oneing of all mankind that shall be saved unto the blessed Trinity. And in these five words God willeth we be enclosed in rest and in peace.

ROBERT: Thank you, dear Lady. Athanasius, I think, would have fallen in love with you — and here, no doubt, he already has. Would it be too much to ask you what you had to say about the question of damnation that seems to be troubling me?

JULIAN: Not at all.

> XXXIII And yet in this I desired, as [far] as I durst, that I might have full sight of Hell and Purgatory. But it was not my meaning to make proof of anything that belongeth to the faith: for I believed soothfastly that Hell and Purgatory is for the same end that Holy Church teacheth, but my meaning was that I might have seen, for learning in all things that belong to my faith, whereby I might live the more to God's worship and to my profit.
>
> But for [all] my desire, I could [see] of this right nought, save as it is aforesaid in the First Shewing, where I saw that the devil is reproved of God and endlessly condemned. In which sight I understood as to all creatures that are of the devil's condition in

this life, and therein end, that there is no more mention made of them afore God and all his Holy than of the devil — notwithstanding that they be of mankind — whether they be christened or not. . . .

And it is God's will that we have great regard to all his deeds that He hath done, but evermore it needeth us to leave the beholding what the Deed shall be. And let us desire to be like our brethren which be saints in Heaven, that will right nought but God's will and are well pleased both with [his] hiding and with [his] shewing. For I saw soothly in our Lord's teaching, the more we busy us to know His secret counsels in this or any other thing, the farther shall we be from the knowing thereof.

ROBERT: Ah! Your kindness skewers us all, good Lady. We chop logic, while you confront us with mystery. I for one am ashamed.

JULIAN: You must not be. I too have felt the same:

XXXV And when God Almighty had shewed me so plenteously and joyfully of His Goodness, I desired to learn assuredly as to a certain creature that I loved, if it should continue in good living, which I hoped by the grace of God was begun. And in this desire for a *singular* shewing, it seemed that I hindered myself: for I was not taught in this time. And then I was answered in my reason, as it were by a friendly intervenor: *Take it* GENERALLY, *and behold the graciousness of the Lord God as He sheweth to thee: for it is more worship to God to behold Him in all than in any special thing . . . for ALL shall be well*. For the fulness of joy is to behold God in *all*: for by the same Might, Wisdom, and Love, that He made all-thing, to the same end our good Lord leadeth it continually, and thereto Himself shall bring it: and when it is time we shall see it. And the ground of this was shewed in the First [Revelation], and more openly in the Third, where it saith: *I saw God in a point.*

ROBERT: Again, the simplicity and humanity of your style stun us — not to mention the depth of your faith. Martin, do you wish to add anything?

LUTHER: I agree with you entirely, Robert; the Lady is a woman after my own heart as well. But if I may (since we've been talking about theological devices here), I'd like to go back to the whole church as a *presence* of Christ, and show you how I tried to avoid giving individual members of the church mediatorial status. In my *Address to the Christian Nobility of the German Nation,* I had this to say:

> As for the unction by a pope or a bishop, tonsure, ordination, consecration, and clothes differing from those of laymen — all this may make a hypocrite or an anointed puppet, but never a Christian or a spiritual man. Thus we are all consecrated as priests by baptism, as St. Peter says: "You are a royal priesthood, a holy nation" (1 Peter 2:9); and in the Book of Revelation: "and you have made us unto our God (by Thy blood) kings and priests" (Revelation 5:10). . . .
>
> And to put the matter more plainly, if a little company of pious Christian laymen were taken prisoners and carried away to a desert, and had not among them a priest consecrated by a bishop, and were there to agree to elect one of them . . . and were to order him to baptize, to celebrate the mass, to absolve and to preach, this man would as truly be a priest, as if all the bishops and all the popes had consecrated him. That is why, in cases of necessity, every man can baptize and absolve, which would not be possible if we were not all priests. This great grace and virtue of baptism and of the Christian estate they have annulled and made us forget by their ecclesiastical law. . . .
>
> For whatever has undergone baptism may boast that it has been consecrated priest, bishop, and pope, although it does not beseem every one to exercise these offices. For, since we are all priests alike, no man may put himself forward, or take upon himself without our consent and election, to do that which we have all alike power to do. . . . And if it should happen that a man were appointed to one of these offices and deposed for abuses, he would be just what he was before. Therefore a priest should be nothing in Christendom but a functionary; as long as he holds his office, he has precedence; if he is deprived of it, he is a peasant or a citizen like the rest. Therefore a priest is verily no

longer a priest after deposition. But now they have invented *characteres indelibiles,* and pretend that a priest after deprivation still differs from a mere layman. They even imagine that a priest can never be anything but a priest — that is, that he can never become a layman. All this is nothing but mere talk and a figment of human imagination.

ROBERT: We're all in your debt, Martin, for your brilliant but alas soon-neglected insight that "we are all consecrated as priests by baptism": the priesthood of all believers was indeed one of the crowning achievements of the Reformation. And I wholeheartedly endorse the way you defend the church's right (by "consent" and "election") to decide when and by whom the *ministerial* function of priesthood can be exercised.

But I wonder. The doctrine of the priesthood of all believers, so plainly declared and confirmed in baptism, eventually fell into the shade even among Protestants. What you said of your own time in your *Babylonish Captivity of the Church* became true of them as well: "There is now scarcely anyone who recalls that he has been baptized since so many other ways have been devised for securing remission of sins and entrance into the kingdom of Heaven." And that situation only got worse with the passage of time. For Lutherans, the word *priest* was too sullied by medieval abuses to be used as an everyday title for Christian ministers (though you yourself didn't hesitate to use it). And as for the other heirs of the Reformation — especially the Anglicans who retained the orders of Deacon, Priest, and Bishop — the more "high church" among them spent most of the nineteenth and twentieth centuries flirting with unreconstructed Roman views of the very "indelible character" of Holy Orders to which you so strenuously object.

So much so, that when the *Concordat* was first proposed in the late 1990s (when Lutherans and Episcopalians were attempting to join forces), the post-Reformation standoffs over deacons, priests, and bishops doomed it. Since I've always been an Anglican (even here, I suppose, that heritage remains part of my glorified history), I still think we could have had it both ways. On the one hand, I see no reason to disagree with Lutherans when they insist that ordination *confers* nothing on priests that their baptism hasn't already said they possessed. Priests don't go to pulpit and altar because they have priestly powers the laity don't have. Priests are an order of *mirrors* set up in the church so that in them, the laity can see their own priestly faces. But on the other hand, as a dyed-in-the-wool Episcopalian I can't quite see what all your fuss over the "indelibility" of priestly ordination was about. Some Lutherans had a panic attack when they heard Anglicans say, "Once a priest, always a priest." But how is that so awful? "Once a parent, always a parent" remains true even if you never speak to your children; "Once a husband, always a husband" holds even after a divorce. Sure, "once an employee of Microsoft, always an employee of Microsoft" won't work, but that's because Microsoft doesn't ordain people (even if it sometimes acts as if it does). Putting people into "orders" simply isn't the same thing as giving them "jobs." Priestly *status* just doesn't equate with ministerial *function*.

So why your rush to say something like "a priest is verily no longer a priest after deposition"? Why do you insist that deposed priests *turn back into* lay persons, when you've made it quite clear that the laity were priests all along? I think I can tell you why. It's because you didn't sufficiently reconstruct the medieval clergy-laity distinction. Your attempt to reform it came a cropper because instead of keeping the spacious image of an *order* in your mind, you tried to make the narrow notion of *employment* do all the work. Let me try to show you what I mean by asking some questions. If I were fired from a job in which I wrote advertising copy, would that loss of employment mean that I lost my status as a member of the sacred order of writers? If not, then why, if I am deprived by the church of my right to be *employed* as a priest, should the church think it must say I've stopped *being* a priest? Or, to put it another way, ordination makes *persons,* not *positions,* the ministerial signs of priesthood. What Gospel imperative is threatened if we continue to call a person without a position a priest? I once lost all my positions in the church and worked as a free-lance writer; but it never occurred to me to think I'd lost my priesthood. If every Christian is a priest by Baptism anyway, isn't it odd to hold that only out-of-work ministers must be deprived of that title?

But I must stop myself. Dame Julian's face may be calm, but the reproach of her words has caught up with me yet again: I wax wroth over things long since swallowed up by the mirth and joy we have in our dear Lord. Anything more, Martin?

LUTHER: I think that my words about the Eucharist (again, in *The Babylonish Captivity*) might fit in here:

> Another scandal must be removed . . . namely the general belief that the mass is a sacrifice which is offered to God. . . . Hence Christ is called the victim of the altar. . . . [And] because they take their stand so obstinately on these grounds we must with equal steadfastness set against them the words of Christ. . . . For in them there is no mention of a "work" or a "sacrifice." . . . The offering of a sacrifice is incompatible with the distribution of a testament or the reception of a promise; the former [the distribution of the New Testament in Christ's blood] we receive, the latter [our embrace of Christ's promise by faith] we give. The same thing cannot be at once received and offered, nor be given and accepted by the same person at the same time.

ROBERT: I have no problems with the substance of what you say, Martin. The Eucharist is not a repetition of the sacrifice of Jesus on the altar of a church; it's a sacramental and real presence of his sacrifice which, because he is present in all times and places, is present everywhere. You're right in saying that Christ is not the "victim of the altar"; he's the Victim of the cross, full stop. Yes, Jesus on Calvary makes a "once and for all" sacrifice; and yes, sacrifice is one of the choicest images for illuminating Jesus' death. But I think you should have been more chary than you were of the medieval tendency to turn even the sacrifice of the cross into a kind of external requirement that Jesus had to fulfill in order to be the Savior of the world. That was another of the doctrinal sleepers the Middle Ages bequeathed to us, and it was one which you allowed to slumber on in your own theology. (So did we all: even in my time, most Christians were still snuggling up with it.)

What fascinates me most about the Eucharist, however, is how little the early fathers had to say about it — even though they unfailingly celebrated it as their principal act of worship every Lord's Day. The arguments about what it meant and how Christ was present in it didn't really begin until the tenth century. But from that day till yours and mine, debate over *doctrines* of the Eucharist (and the requirement of "correct" doctrine before people could take part in it) so mesmerized the church that when the age-old *practice* of Eucharist every Sunday gave way to a non-Eucharistic preaching service, hardly anyone complained. Only in the last half of the twentieth century did we (thanks to the liturgical movement, not the theologians) start taking Jesus' command to "do this" seriously again. Only then did we reclaim the church of the fathers.

Nonetheless, I'd like for us to end on a higher note than that, so I'm going to ask Dame Julian if she'll oblige us. Madam, do you think you might move our minds as far upstairs as our bodies now are?

JULIAN: I shall try.

V In this same time our Lord shewed me a ghostly sight of His homely loving.

I saw that He is to us everything that is good and comfortable for us: He is our clothing that for love wrappeth us, claspeth us, and all becloseth us for tender love, that He may never leave us; being to us all-thing that is good, as to my understanding.

Also in this He shewed me a little thing, the quantity of an hazel-nut, in the palm of my hand; and it was as round as a ball. I looked thereupon with the eye of my understanding and thought: *What may this be?* And it was answered generally thus: *It is all that is made.* I marvelled how it might last, for methought it might suddenly have fallen to naught for little[ness]. And I was answered in my understanding: *It lasteth, and ever shall [last] for that God loveth it.* And so All-thing hath the Being by the love of God. . . .

Also our Lord God shewed that it is full great pleasance to Him that a helpless soul come to Him simply and plainly and homely. For this is the natural yearnings of the soul, by the

142

touching of the Holy Ghost (as by the understanding that I have in this Shewing): *God, of Thy Goodness, give me Thyself: for Thou art enough to me, and I may nothing ask that is less than may be full worship to Thee; and if I ask anything that is less, ever me wanteth but only in Thee I have all.*

And these words are full lovely to the soul, and full near touch they the will of God and His Goodness. For His Goodness comprehendeth all His creatures and all his blessed works, and overpasseth without end. For He is the endlessness, and He hath made us only to Himself, and restored us by His blessed Passion, and keepeth us in His blessed love; and all this of His Goodness.

ROBERT: Alleluia! And Amen! Now for the Macallan!

ALL: Alleluia, Amen, *und Ein Prosit!*

EIGHT

Where It All Took Us

I n this final chapter I'm going to revisit the subject of the Bible itself. But this time, I'll confine myself to only one aspect of it: the
historical side effects of the Reformers' attempts to restore Scripture to its rightful place in the life of the church. I want to talk with
you about what I'll call their "originalism": their campaign to make
the Bible alone the sacred original of all truth.

Their first step on that crusade was quite appropriate. They insisted that the church had no right to teach anything which couldn't
be founded on the Word of God revealed in Scripture. Unfortunately,
though, there was a sleeper in that. It contained a lurking implication
that the title "Word of God" belonged primarily to the Bible and not
to Jesus himself as the Word Incarnate. The Reformers, of course,
never wavered in their commitment to the Incarnation. But all their
talk about the Bible as the church's sole source for faith in Jesus
(something it couldn't possibly have been, since the faith of the earliest church predated the entire New Testament) upset the balance between church and Scripture. In the Old Testament, as I've said, the
scriptural accounts arose from within the community of faith, not
the other way around. And in the New Testament, it isn't the biblical
record that validates Jesus; it's Jesus who validates the biblical record.
But the mischief didn't stop there: their successors took a second and
more questionable step. When doubts later arose about the reliability
of the biblical deposit itself, they decided to rummage through that

sacred original for a Jesus behind the Jesus of Scripture, a more "historical" Jesus who they hoped would be more reliable than the one who happened to stand on the pages of the New Testament.

The stages before that second step, however, were hardly as problematical. In fact, they were positively beneficial. By going back from the Latin of the Vulgate to the original Hebrew and Greek, the Reformers produced more reliable texts. In short, they quite rightly invented textual criticism of the Bible; and on the basis of those better texts, they translated it into the languages of their time. Prior to the Reformation, the Scriptures had indeed been a *voice* within the church rather than a book delivered to the church. In the Middle Ages, of course, it hadn't been a very good voice. It spoke in a language most listeners couldn't comprehend; and when it might have been heard from pulpits, the rank and file of preachers who were supposed to be its tongues hardly knew it any better than the laity. (The Reformers fixed that too. They put the liturgy as well as the Scriptures into a "language understanded of the people"; and they insisted on sermons from the text of Scripture itself rather than preachments about such matters as buying indulgences, going on pilgrimages, and the observance of ecclesiastically imposed fasts — none of which were to be found in the Bible.) But there was a troublesome side effect of the Reformers' invention of "biblical criticism."

The Bible as the only sacred original tended to become a thing in its own right, a sovereign resource that more and more came to be seen as standing over against the church. This was not totally bad, of course. Scripture does have a sovereignty of its own; but then, so does the apostolic witness of the church. On any fair view, the Bible should be seen as jointly authoritative with the church. To be sure, when and if the church violates the apostolic witness of the Scriptures, it should be corrected by that witness. But only so it can be recalled to its own true apostolicity, not so it can derive that attribute from a book. However, before I go on to say what else went wrong in the post-Reformation handling of the Bible, let me put a longish note in your pocket so you'll have an orderly checklist to set against the less than sequential ramble through my subjects that I now propose to take you on.

∿

The SIXTEENTH CENTURY was a time of history-making, even earth-shaking upheavals. In addition to the arrival of printed books the century before, it witnessed the rise of the nation-states of Europe. It saw the adaptation of the medieval notion of a single "Christendom" to those newly powerful principalities (thus producing mini-Christendoms all over the map). Along those same lines, it invented the "divine right of kings," with its concomitant principle that the ruler alone could determine the religion of his people *(cuius regio, eius religio)*. And it experienced the beginnings of confessionalism (the Augsburg Confession, the Heidelberg Catechism, the Thirty-nine Articles, the Creed of Pius the Fifth, and the rest), the discovery and exploration of the New World, the development of commerce, and the eventual colonization of non-European lands. But that was only the beginning.

The SEVENTEENTH CENTURY brought with it the flowering of the physical sciences (with Newton, for example), the dissolution of Christendom's unity in the chaos of national religions (all Scots had to be Presbyterian, all Englishmen, C. of E., and so on), the challenging of the divine right of kings (by Locke and Hobbes, among others), the beginnings of the Enlightenment (same crew), the start of the quest for the historical Jesus, and the exportation of the state religions recently developed within more hospitable old-world limits to a virtually frontierless America.

The EIGHTEENTH CENTURY saw the rank growth of Deism with its skepticism about miracles and its image of creation as a perfectly made watch that needed no further adjustments by God, the coming of age of the philosophical doubt that was only a toddler in the previous century, the beginnings of evolutionism (Laplace), the first stirrings of the Industrial Revolution, the creation of a new politics based on the inalienable rights of individual human beings, and of course, the great American experiments with the Declaration of Independence, the Constitution, and the Bill of Rights.

The NINETEENTH CENTURY marked the aggrandizement of higher criticism, the abolition of slavery, the death throes of the Christendom ideal (the Catholic Emancipation Act in England, for

146

example), the flourishing of the missionary movement and the attendant chauvinism of the "white man's burden," the maturation of an industrial economy, the political advocacy of women's rights, the outbreak of the clash between science and religion, the philosophical ascendancy of Darwinism, the burgeoning of determinism, the rebirth of the corporation as a private enterprise and of its twin, the corporate model of the church, the continued growth of racism, and the creation of modern warfare.

And the TWENTIETH CENTURY — perhaps now late-lamented, if anyone can shed a tear for such a time of incredible progress and abysmal decline — witnessed what most of us know too well. On the ecclesiastical side, we invented Fundamentalism; on the right, we fell in love with literalism, and on the left, we retreated into the cul-de-sac of an "ethical" Jesus and a "social" Gospel; we applauded the rise of Neo-orthodoxy in Barth as a reaction against both of those; we created alternative theologies to Barth (Niebuhr, Tillich, process theology, feminist theology, liberation theology); we hailed the ecumenical movement — but all of those achievements were a mixed bag of good intentions and questionable results. And on the secular side, we saw similar outcomes. We saw the invention of aircraft and wars of increasing senselessness. We bought better things for better living, and we had lives that were not lived as well. We watched the wonder of television and complained about the wasteland of TV....

∼

But enough. If that omnium-gatherum note has failed to mention dozens of things it should have, I apologize. Back to my subject in this chapter.

As I look over that list of historic developments, an image occurs to me. It's a picture of the God of history rolling one bowling ball after another at the human race's well-laid designs for renovations that never quite turned out as anyone planned. Many brilliant people did many brilliant things through all those years; but what they did was regularly bowled over by other things they couldn't possibly have seen coming. "Man proposes, God disposes," goes the old saying. That's never been more true than in the almost five hundred years since the Reformation — and it was certainly never more un-predictably true than in that period's attitudes toward the Scriptures and their role in the life of the church. I realize, of course, that nobody ever saw the Divine Bowler actually putting hand to ball. But since the balls themselves were visible enough in history, I want to see if we can detect any fingerprints God may have left on them.

As far as the sixteenth century is concerned, some of the prints are unmistakably God's: Scripture was restored to its place of honor in the church, the church itself was renewed as a community of faith, and grace was re-established as the only operative factor in the salvation of the world. Admittedly, there were also other finger-prints on those balls. God may be the owner of the bowling alley of history, but he lets human beings join the games when and as they choose. Sometimes he leaves them free to play as they can and simply puts up with their less-than-divine scores: he didn't ban Luther for bowling poorly on the subject of ministerial priesthood, nor did he evict Calvin for reckless endangerment with the ball of predestination. But at other times, God seems to have thrown some of the questionable balls himself: he didn't just put up with them; he turned their very waywardness into an impetus for their eventual correction. Maybe that's what he was doing when he allowed the medieval fascination with propositional theology to go unreformed, knowing that it would soon enough lead to the excesses of confessionalism, and that the confessions would in turn bring on disenchantment with propositional theology *tout court* — and that then, perhaps, the twentieth century would get sick of theology as a question-answering game and get back to throwing strikes instead of gutter balls.

That's getting ahead of ourselves, though. Let me take you on a slightly longer rumination through those centuries and see if I can fill in some of the gaps.

The seventeenth century obviously bears a good many marks of the hand of the Divine Suspect. For one thing, it began to edge minds away from at least some of the Reformers' preoccupations. The invention of religious liberty was a step away from Luther's mistake in siding with the rulers of German states rather than with the peasants who were his natural allies. Newton's attention to the laws of nature (and of nature's God) foreshadowed the eventual freeing of thought from the shackles of a Bible presumed to teach science. And the creation of higher criticism — beginning with the quest for the historical Jesus at the end of the 1600s, and despite the later blind alleys into which it led the church — was at least a move toward seeing that God reveals himself in the rough-and-tumble of history, not in the niceties of theological overlays on it.

But since other hands than God's were definitely on that last ball, I want to make a few comments on where I think the higher — as opposed to the merely textual — critics went wrong.

Printing may have made the Bible a thing in its own right; but it also led to a debate over precisely what kind of thing it was. By and large, the seventeenth century never doubted that it was some sort of whole — that for all its diversity, it possessed a unity of content and purpose. There was, however, considerable disagreement about the nature of that wholeness. Was it a unity like that of any other well-crafted book, or was it something greater (or less) than that? Were all the parts of the whole absolutely correct and binding, or could some of them be seen as erroneous and dispensable? Again (to use some images from later times), was its unity organic or inorganic? And if it was organic, could portions of its wholeness be amputated with impunity, or was it one-celled, as it were, and would it be in danger of death on the operating table? And finally (to bring the imagery all the way up-to-date), if Scripture was indeed an organic whole, did it become that because the Spirit inserted some holy DNA to regulate every aspect of its being, or did the accidents of its history also have a role to play? Could you (to come to my point at last) *clone* the whole from bits and pieces?

My answer to that last one is, I don't think so. But in order to help you see why, I have another home-brewed image of Scripture to show you: the image of a *party* thrown by the Holy Spirit as its Host. Do you see what that one does? No one can clone an original party simply by inviting some (or even all) of the previous guests to a repeat performance. (When I was a priest in the Hamptons on Long Island, the rich and famous tried that gambit over and over; but all it ever produced was a second party worse than the first.) A party is a meeting of persons; and persons are not just creatures who spend their lives fulfilling the destiny of their genes. Their history contributes as much to their being as their heredity. Even identical twins develop different personalities: however slight the variations in their subsequent circumstances might be, those are quite sufficient to produce personal twoness out of genetic oneness. (You can't clone Einstein as a person from an earlobe or a blood sample because you can't manage to put his gene copy through the exact historical conditions of Einstein's life.) And therefore every wise host knows that each party is a fresh risk, not a sure thing. The same parts can never make the same party.

So too with the party of Scripture — and with the Spirit as its Host. He invites radically free persons to it, not just creatures he's pre-ordained to echo his views. He doesn't dictate their histories; he accepts them and revels in their vagaries. Unfortunately, the heirs of the Reformation didn't have the benefit of that happy image; instead, they had a darker one that brewed trouble for them. It was the deterministic image suggested by Calvin's inscrutably predestinarian and therefore totally managerial God. And when they applied that controlling view of God's will to the divine management of Scripture, it played hob with the historicity of the Bible. It led a good many of them to insist that everything in the sacred original was to be taken as literal truth from the mouth of God. If Scripture said that Adam died at the age of 930, that had to be taken at face value because the basic principle of biblical interpretation was riding on it. If it said that the rabbit chewed the cud, or if it showed Jesus ascending from two different places, no one was allowed to balk at those contradictions for the same reason. And if it assigned barbarities to the Deity — as it did when the LORD attempted to murder Moses in an inn (Exod. 4:24), or when "the anger of the LORD was kindled against Uzzah; and God smote him there [for his innocent touching of the ark of the LORD]; and there he died by the ark of God" (2 Sam. 6:6-11) — then those short-tempered fits of mayhem had to be considered as much a revelation of God's heart of hearts as the death and resurrection of his Son.

In fairness, it must be said that the Reformers themselves never went that far. They felt quite free to assign other senses than the merely literal to scriptural passages that gave them pause. They could, as the church long had, escape from historical or ethical binds by resorting to allegorical, spiritual, or mystical interpretations. Luther was even so bold as to try escaping from an entire book: he called the letter of James an "Epistle of straw." But once the Calvinist notion of a God unanswerable for bad behavior took root in people's attitudes toward Scripture, literalism — conceived of as the only sense in which the Bible could be read — was only a few miles down the road, waiting to scare the bejeezus out of anyone who hoped (by Jesus) that God was love. The church at large, of course, did resist the literalists' sales pitches for a good while. (It wasn't until the late nineteenth and early twentieth centuries that entire denominations began buying into literalism.) But once that sale had been made, far too many Christians found their purchase hard to part with. Even now, it's still cherished as the only key to the Scriptures.

But there is no such single key, and higher criticism deserves credit for recognizing that fact, at least at its beginning. The critics felt that if God saved the world in the thick of its history, they could consider themselves free to test even the historicity of the Bible itself by challenging passages previously interpreted as historical fact. In doing so, however, they frequently fell into the trap of trying to unlock biblical history by means of other keys that were no better than literalism. As the eighteenth and nineteenth centuries continued their march toward disbelief in miracles and denial of the Incarnation, the higher critics marched right along. If Deism would allow God no personal intervention in history because it saw the world as a self-sufficient piece of clockwork, then they would prune the miraculous out of the Bible. If their theological contemporaries saw Jesus as nothing but a man, then they would follow suit and write off passages that said he was God as well — thus booting pretty much the entire Gospel of John out of the canon. So when they came to evaluate the Bible as a whole, the critics decided that much of the "real" history in the Bible had been covered over with the opinions of a more credulous age — prescientific notions, mythologizing tendencies — which had been rendered irrelevant by more enlightened views. (*Myth* isn't all bad, of course: as a way of introducing images into theological discourse, it's positively useful.) But as most people heard the word "demythologizing," they thought the critics were saying that if only the theological overlays on Scripture could be peeled away, a truer Jesus, more acceptable to modern minds, would be revealed.

The peeling, though, turned out to be a false start. It was an enterprise that left them with a Jesus who was little more than a teacher of ethics. Such ethicism, however, was simply the other side of the coin of literalism; both of those -isms were simply a refuge from the untidiness with which Scripture presents us. If what you say about the Bible is "Every word of it is literally true," then you please conservative minds; if your watchword is "Only its moral teachings are to be taken as revelation," then you please liberal minds. But either way, you're still under the curse of literalistic originalism. Nor does it advance our understanding of the Bible if you urge that we abandon the "cosmic Christ of Paul" for the "simple Jesus of the Gospels." The Gospels are no less "propaganda" than the letters of Paul: both give us the Person of Jesus in the clothing of theological interpretation. Nevertheless, the New Testament — and the whole of the Old Testament, for that matter — are the sole records we have of the presence of the Word Incarnate in history. *The Bible remains the only historical costume in which Jesus appears to us.* Stripping off parts of his clothing in the hope of revealing a more authentic Jesus is not peeling some fuzzy skin off an otherwise perfect peach; it's messing with the very Person of the only Peach we have. The Scriptures are precisely a costume party. Depriving the honored Guest of even a smitch of the outfit he's worn to the festivities is the last thing the Host wants us to do.

As a matter of fact, it now occurs to me that the Bible is a *series* of costume parties — a whole long season of them in which the Word made flesh appears to us in many disguises. The Four Gospels may be the affairs at which the Guest of Honor is most easily recognized; but Paul's epistles, Colossians, and Ephesians are no less splendid affairs. And the rest of the Bible is right up there with all the other celebrations in its presentation of the Principal Person of Scripture. So it isn't just that there's a single, New Testament party of the Incarnation to which the Old Testament simply gives us allegories or comparisons; there are many parties (in both Testaments), and the same Incarnate Word makes a personal appearance at all of them.

It's a bad idea, therefore, to imagine that the Incarnation took place only once in history, early in the first century. What we should be trying to do is recognize Christ in all the costumes he put on no matter which parties he wore them to. The Paschal Lamb, the Pillars of Cloud and Fire, the Rock in the Wilderness, and the Manna from Heaven are each of them the Word himself. They're all sacraments of his presence in creation from beginning to end — and others of them are even signs of his existence before the beginning and after the end (the Word by whom all things are made, the Life that is the Light of all humanity, and the Son of man who comes to judge the living and the dead, and who reigns for ever and ever). But, like all sacraments, they're outward and visible signs that disguise his hidden presence as much as they reveal it. The mind can see only the costumes; it takes faith to recognize the Person.

In fact, disguising himself is the Word's choicest way of disclosing himself. Even during his earthly career as the Person of Jesus' humanity — through those thirty-three years when he was most recognizable as a Somebody rather than an abstract divine principle or an allegorical device — he still went out of his way to hide. Running away from people was practically a compulsion with him. He frequently left the disciples and went off to pray by himself; and he often absented himself from people he'd just helped (like the man born blind in John 9). Then there was his habit of telling those who did manage to recognize him not to reveal his "secret." (He commanded the demons who knew who he was to be silent; and after Peter said "You are the Messiah," he warned his friends that "they should speak to nobody about him.") But that habit of hiding was manifest long before the Word revealed Himself in Jesus of Nazareth. In the Old Testament, the Person of the Word disguised himself in costumes that didn't even look like persons (Pillar, Water, Manna). When he finally did reveal his Incarnation in Jesus, he carried his hiding still further. He concealed his divine power in the weakness of an infant, his creating voice in thirty years of saying next to nothing, his immortality as God the Son in his death on the cross, and his reconciliation of all history in a resurrection that repaired not a scrap of its ongoing disaster.

But there's a snare laid in all that hiding. Unwary interpreters can easily be led to conclude that the Incarnation of the Word of God was an event which occurred only in one particular time and place, and thus limit the Word's becoming flesh to Jesus alone. Now it's certainly true that the masked ball of Jesus' life on earth was the grandest of all the parties at which the Word himself showed up: we can never pay too much attention to it. But by the same token, if he was present at every preceding and subsequent party, we're duty bound to try and recognize him in those as well. We're not allowed to turn the climactic party into the only party. And we're just as forbidden to treat the others as if they were simply predictions of a party yet to come — merely mental anticipations of an Incarnation that would be inserted as a fact of history at some later date.

Indeed, I think that this insertional view of the Incarnation was one of the faulty interpretive setups of biblical bowling pins which God was aiming at when he rolled many of the balls we've been talking about. I've labeled those mistaken rearrangements of the scriptural narrative "transactionalism" — and by now you're probably sick of hearing that clumsy word. But by any other name, the bad habit of seeing the Incarnation as something poked into history at one point, and not as the very ground of history, has been around for a long time. Even Irenaeus and Athanasius, despite all their insistence on the Person of the Word as the reconciler of history, still tended to speak of his Incarnation as if it were a single historical event that had cosmic ramifications rather than a cosmic fact that had many historical manifestations.

Furthermore, later interpreters mired themselves deeper and deeper in that misapprehension. From the Middle Ages to the present, the gift of the Incarnation has been seen as something transferred from Jesus to us (by the church, or by faith, or by predestination, or by imputation) rather than as something already in everybody by the presence of the Word who makes and sustains the whole creation. And hence God's bowling balls. The course of higher criticism — from Reimarus to Wrede, from the late seventeenth century to the Jesus Seminar — has been one long, divine shake-up of the way we've handled history and Scripture. That we still haven't gotten all the pins reset as they should be may be unfortunate; but since God has been throwing balls at us for two thousand years, I have a hunch he's in no hurry: he'll just go on rolling till we do.

As a matter of fact, the very first instances of his bowling can be instructive for us. When he threw Paul and Colossians at the Jerusalem church, he knocked apart an entire view of history. James and company had assumed that since they were proclaiming the fulfillment of Jewish history in Jesus the Messiah, they had to perpetuate the exclusivity of Jewish history in their church. (The Gentiles, being outside Judaism, had to become Jews by circumcision and observance of the dietary laws before they could be members of the new community.) But Paul was God's instrument for disrupting that notion. He pointed out that Abraham became the "father of a great people" by faith in God's promise, not by the law which came 430 years later. And Colossians continued the shake-up, insisting that in the circumcision of Jesus the whole world had been circumcised with a circumcision not made with hands.

I repeat that here because it applies nicely to my view that God's vision of history is not blinkered, as ours so often is, by historical sequence. He's present in and to the entire sweep of history, and all of that sweep is present in and to him. He doesn't have to wait for history to happen, nor does history have to wait for him to show up. But at the risk of yet another repetition, I want to bring back the Gospel according to John as God's pre-eminent ball for breaking up the restrictions of our linear view of history. In his prologue, John expounds the Incarnation not by tying it to the narratives of Jesus' birth but by going all the way back to the beginning of everything. "In the beginning was the Word," he says, "and the Word was with God, and the Word was God. . . . All things were made by him. . . . And the Word became flesh and dwelt among us."

Do you see what that says? It says that the time-bound creation ("all things") is restored by the Word who is beyond time even while he's right in the middle of it — and who therefore can show up in as many different times as he pleases. John's Gospel has often (especially in recent centuries) been written off as non-historical. But what a whopping misunderstanding that is when in fact it's the one Gospel which has a vision of history as something more than pearls on a necklace. I even think John was quite conscious of this. His re-

155

arrangements of the sequences in the Synoptic Gospels are auda-
cious. For instance, he transfers Jesus' cleansing of the temple from
its position in the other Gospels (after the triumphal entry into Jerusalem) to the beginning of Jesus' ministry. And then there are his
strange omissions of events in the Synoptic histories — such as the
Institution of the Eucharist, for which he substitutes the dialogue
at Capernaum after the feeding of the five thousand (John 6). This
suggests a deeper view of God's way with history than the image of a
line of cars stuck in traffic on the freeway.

John, you see, just wasn't proclaiming a transactional Incarnation; and I don't think he was simply trying to correct the other
Gospel writers' "historical" errors. He was breaking new ground in
the soil of history-writing itself. He was leading us to recognize the
enfleshed Word who had been in history from the start. He was calling us to stop being detectives on Jesus' case and to become lovers
who can recognize him wherever he may hide. For John — and for
Irenaeus, Athanasius, and a host of others at their best — the enterprise is not to strip the Word of his biblical costume; it's to fall so in
love with him that no matter what his disguises, we can say, "I'd
know him anywhere."

Admittedly, there's a trap even in that more liberating view of
biblical history. It's easy to let it turn the Jesus of history into just
another instance of something more fundamental than Jesus. You
start out by talking about the Incarnation of the Word; but then
you go on to make the abstract idea of incarnation the main subject
and turn Jesus into an avatar of it. In short, you put the cart of what
the Word did before the Horse of the Person he is. But that's not
what I have in mind at all. And what saves me from it is precisely the
fact that there's only one such Person throughout the whole Bible.
Both the Paschal Lamb and Jesus of Nazareth are the Word himself
made flesh. None of the costumes the Word put on should be identified as anything but the Word himself. Not one of them should be
seen as a mere stand-in for something else.

If my wife Valerie, for example, chooses (as she often does) to try
on fourteen outfits before she finally selects her dinner dress,
should I say that I've seen nothing but avatars of something other
than Valerie? Were all those changes of clothing only "well-dressed-

womanness" appearing in the guise of my wife? Was only her last choice the "real" Valerie? Did the first fourteen give me nothing but intimations of her? Of course not. Wouldn't it be better to say that my wife just likes to put on disguises and never left our bedroom during the whole performance? Like God, she does this all the time; but I learned long ago that trying to impose my preferences on the situation gets me nowhere fast. My only business with either of them is to love and tag along.

If I may extend that insight a bit, I even think it enables me to say a kind word about Calvin. In retrospect, some of my harshness with him has been due to my own misunderstanding. It now seems to me that he too realized the benefits of just loving the Word of God and tagging along. Valerie's grooming dalliances are not the only thing I've been learning to put up with for the sake of Valerie. Sometimes, in a fit of depression, she'll do or say the most reprehensible things. At least they seem so to me: as a devout narcissist, I have a deep conviction that I shouldn't have to put up with vituperation. My first reaction is to protest that I'm a nice person — which she takes as an accusation against her and proceeds to let all hell break loose. My second is to withdraw — which only puts off the fire and brimstone to a later and longer session of recrimination. And my third and worst response is to become nasty myself — thus blowing my claim to what little niceness I may have. Simple, tag-along love is the only thing that has even a chance of making things better.

So too, I think, with John Calvin. The God of Scripture, like it or not, seems to have had quite a few bouts of depression — complete with what can only be called fits of superhuman meanness. In light of that insight, I no longer think that Calvin got some kind of kick out of consigning a huge chunk of humanity to eternal fire. I just think that, for whatever reasons, he decided to take his Scripture neat, and as a lover himself, to put up with his Lover's inscrutable behavior. After all, the difference between God's extermination of the innocent Uzzah and his predestining of throngs to eternal death is one of degree, not of kind. Both are terrible; but if you love a person (even the Divine Person of the Word), you put up with everything and take your lumps. True enough, later Calvinism tried to justify even God's day-of-judgment nastiness, and later objectors to

157

Calvinism dumped predestination (probably because they were crypto-narcissists). But old John himself just swallowed hard and didn't put niceness between himself and his Lover.

~

I'm going to round off this desultory treatment of the last four hundred years of biblical interpretation by going back once again to the Jesus Seminar.

You no doubt recall how it operated. The Seminar gathered together Scripture scholars to discuss the Gospels, and they debated whether this or that passage could pass muster as the real, or "historical," words of Jesus. Finally, they indicated their judgment of each passage by an intriguing method: each of them voted by casting a colored ball into a container: a red ball meant that a passage was almost certainly authentic; a pink one, that it was possibly authentic; a green one, that it was probably inauthentic; and a black one, that it was almost certainly not the real thing. Then they tallied up the colors, and the one that represented the most votes was declared to be the judgment of the group. But I should stipulate that their printed version of the Gospels gave me more than theological problems. Not because they left any passages out, mind you; just because I'm red-green colorblind. The red printer's ink they chose was a shade I could easily recognize, and the black . . . well, black is a universal experience. But the pink and the green were all but indistinguishable by me: I had to keep pestering Valerie to tell me which was which — and even she, with perfect color perception, sometimes had to struggle for an answer.

All that to one side, I have no profound objections to what the Seminar was trying to do. It seems to me a reasonably pleasant way of arguing about whether Jesus could actually have said the things the Bible said he did. It was rather like a group of bar habitués one-upping each other with stories of their wives' difficult outbursts — which is relatively harmless fun as long as it just lets them get complaints off their chests. But if it goes further than that — if it leads someone to go home and tell his wife he's divorcing her (or, in the case of the Seminar, to deciding that green or black passages should be divorced from the Bible) — authentic damage can be done.

Since the Seminar did end up printing the Gospels in their entirety, it's probably unfair to accuse them of going that far. At least they loved their wife enough to go along with the substance of her being and change only the colors she wore. But if I'm willing to pass only mild judgment on their handling of Scripture, there have been others who weren't, both on the left and on the right. Think of all the "at last we've gotten back to the real Jesus" *schwärmerei* in certain liberal quarters. Think of the "it's nothing but the work of the devil" alarms in conservative circles. And, above all, think of all the bewildered pastors who have asked their visiting lecturer to reassure them that the ultimate poison pill hasn't been dropped into the scriptural soup — and who wonder out loud whether they can still preach on the almost entirely black-letter Gospel of John that the church still hands them on so many Sundays.

It was that last one, I think, that was the real danger in all the hoo-ha about the Jesus Seminar. Preachers are not ordained on the basis of their ability to justify their sermons by critical standards. They're ordained to fall in love with the exasperating Jesus of Bible and church, and to move their hearers to do the same. In the course of that enterprise, they might possibly consider themselves free to question whether this or that Gospel writer understood Jesus as well as some other biblical author did. And certainly, they might want to put an interpretive arm on some of Jesus' words because others strike them as more central to his message or identity. But at all times they must remember that they're wives and husbands of Scripture: they may complain all they like about their spouse's foibles; but they may never assume that the marriage is over. The Bible is the church's spouse for life. The fact that some of it may give us *tsouris*, or *agita*, or second thoughts, is no reason for giving any of it the gate.

∾

But whatever the case may be with the members of the Jesus Seminar — or with their audience — I still think that the whole history of biblical interpretation has always been, and will always be, covered with the fingerprints of God. The Father has imprinted it all with his good pleasure in the Beloved Son who indwells every episode of it. The Incarnate Word, in all his guises (early or late, fetching or not), remains the star of the show who has left at least the mark of his thumb on every act. And the Holy Spirit has handled it so thoroughly that the whole of it bears witness to the "Finger of the Hand Divine," who never wrote anything but the same old story: *All shall be well, and all shall be well, and all manner of thing shall be well.* The only thing we need to do is gaze long enough at those fingerprints to trust the three Persons who left them — and then to let our love answer theirs as best we can.

EPILOGUE

Fact, Fiction, and Truth

I admit that I've given you a quirky book. But its oddity lies not so much in its conclusions (which are my usual mix of conservatism and liberalism, if you have to use those labels) as it does in my antic habit of playing with images in front of audiences who'd rather have straight talk. Your own opinions of my performance, of course, have been formed by now. They may range from encomiums that find me "fresh, charming, and brilliant," to cavils that charge me with being "repetitive, confusing, over the top, and shallow to boot"; or they may go all the way down to condemnations that write me off as "dead wrong and too full of himself by half." But whatever they are, I neither apologize nor explain. I simply say "Very good!" and let them go at that. In these last pages, I just want to take exception to your charge that I'm too full of myself by half.

I could easily object that no author worth his salt would write a word unless he was brash enough to think he had something to add to what's been said before by "men whom one cannot hope to emulate." But I won't go down that road. Instead, I shall give you a short disquisition on what I see as flaws in your understanding of the relationship between fact, fiction, and truth. And I particularly want to do that since I've apparently not said clearly enough that both fact and fiction can be equally true. Let me try to put it another way.

All human beings possess the truth of their own existence as a fact, no matter how much or little of that truth they may succeed in expressing. (Actually, they can never get any of it completely right: even casual acquaintances know us better than we know ourselves.) But more to the point, all writers fictionalize themselves when they sit down to put words into a book. The writer of a biography, for example (even one who professes to be "objective"), is a fictional character on the pages of his book. Even if he scrupuously tries to stay out of the reader's way, the person he thus hides is still a person he has made up — no less so than the glorious or grimy character which the writer of an autobiography hands us as his "true" self. No whole or true or "historical" person ever appears in print. All we get from any writer is one human mind's radically limited — if not downright false — picture of somebody who exists only in his head.

That goes for Thomas Aquinas, who projects so little ego into his works that he might as well be a theological CD-ROM. It goes for Julian of Norwich, who injects so much of herself into her *Revelations of Divine Love* that she becomes a persistent sweetheart trying to extract reassurance after reassurance from Jesus. It even goes for the human Jesus, who was wrestling with the biggest ego of them all, the Person of the Word of God, and who, on the evidence of Scripture, sometimes seems not to have gotten that fact into his human mind. ("My God, my God, why have you forsaken me?" is only the most dramatic illustration.)

And so it most certainly goes for the Robert you've met in this book. He too is a work of fiction. If you don't understand him or like him, be comforted. Neither do I. That Robert, right along with me even in my best moments, has only a nodding acquaintance with the real one. Half of what he thinks he understands he's gotten wrong; and most of what he thinks he likes is not all that likable. We know in part and we prophesy in part. We're simply marking mental time until the day when we'll know ourselves as we've been known — with luck, by others here; but with certainty, by Somebody Else who's known us fully all along.

That doesn't mean the truth about us is unavailable to us. From Adam, to Jesus, to you, and to me, we've all had the privilege of being. (As Aquinas pointed out, there's no ontological falsehood: whatever we are, and however ignorantly or mendaciously we conceive ourselves in our own minds, we stand in the truth of our own being as it exists in the mind and the speaking of God.) But it does mean we won't uncover that truth by scraping away the fictionalizations by which we, or the Scriptures, have tried to present it. Those fictions *are* that truth in its only available form for us now. If you don't like the Robert of this book, or the Jesus of Scripture, you're free to look for another you might like better. But remember: no matter who else you find in this vale of half-truths, you'll only get a different set of fictions.

The business of poetry, Marianne Moore said, is to give us "imaginary gardens with real toads in them." For me, that solves all the problems of biblical criticism. It doesn't matter if many flowers in the Gospel garden are the imaginings — the imagings — of first-century minds; the True Frog of Jesus is hiding in that shrubbery, waiting to astonish us with his leaps and bounds. And it doesn't matter if other parts of Scripture, or even great swatches of it, are the imagings of John, Matthew, Paul, or Jesus himself. The Holy Spirit was pleased to let their imagery stand *wie es steht geschrieben* — as it lies before us — in the one and only Bible we have. The Spirit, like a good poet, knows that metaphors, analogies, and images are not only the best tools we're going to find for getting at the truth — they're the only ones. Nor does it make any difference if all the dancers at the ball of images (authors and characters alike) were full or empty of themselves, or of any fraction thereof. If they were selves at all, they could express that truth no better way than by making their froggy impersonations, fact or fiction, as real as possible.

There's just no other path from the mystery of our being to the truth of our condition. And there are no other guides than folks just like us to point out that road. If even the Way himself lost his way for our sakes, who are we to wish the Bible were a better map? All we need do is follow, as best we can, the Road Atlas we already have.

So once again, "Very good!" — and another *Prosit!* By the grace of God, we'll see each other in the Divine Suspect at the end of the journey.